CRITTER CHAT

What if ANIMALS used SOCIAL MEDIA?

ROSEMARY MOSCO

NATIONAL GEOGRAPHIC
Washington, D.C.

PSST—WATCH THIS BIRD!

The arctic tern migrates from the Arctic to the Antarctic Peninsula every year. That's a really, really long journey. As you read this book, the tern may show up in some ... unexpected places.

So keep your eyes open and see how often you can spot her!

CRITTER CHAT

ARCTIC TERN

LIVES IN: The Arctic in the summertime
(later, she'll travel to the Antarctic!)
SCREEN NAME: TernAround

FRIENDS

OneToothWonder
Narwhal

Hoofs_N_Horns
Musk ox

FurryFiend
Arctic fox

TernAround
Summertime is coming to an end! How has everybody's summer been? I caught a ton of fish, so my summer terned out just fine.

Hoofs_N_Horns
I'm busy raising my calf. She was born just a few weeks ago, and she's got wide hooves, just like me!
#ProudMuskoxMama

OneToothWonder
Congrats on the new kiddo! I'm slapping my flukes in excitement.

FurryFiend
Pfft. ONE calf? That's nothing. I'm raising SIX pups, and I'm EXHAUSTED.

TURN PAGE

TernAround

I'm obsessed with my current look. But in winter, I'll mix things up with a black beak and a lighter-colored forehead. What's your summer style?

OneToothWonder

My eight-foot (2.4-m) spiral tooth is always in style. *#TimelessTooth*

Hoofs_N_Horns

Summer? I'm already working on growing the extra-thick coat that'll keep me warm in the winter!

FurryFiend

Pfft. That's NOTHING. My WHOLE COAT changes from white in winter to brown in summer. It's EXHAUSTING being this trendy.

TernAround
Ugh. I love hanging out with all of you, but it's time for me to fly to my wintering grounds.

Hoofs_N_Horns
Where are you going?

TernAround
The other side of the planet: Antarctica!

FurryFiend
Pfft, that's NOTHING. I—wait. Actually, that's a really impressive trip. Wow. How will you even survive? I'm tired just thinking about it.

TernAround
Um, thanks, I guess. See you when I return!

Dolphinstagram

platypus
📍 Eastern Australia

SELFIE!

❤️ **54 likes**

platypus I'm an egg-cellent mom! That's because I'm one of the only mammals that lays eggs. I keep my eggs warm for 10 days until they hatch. Incubating: It's not just for the birds. #MomLife

11

ANIMAL INFLUENCER

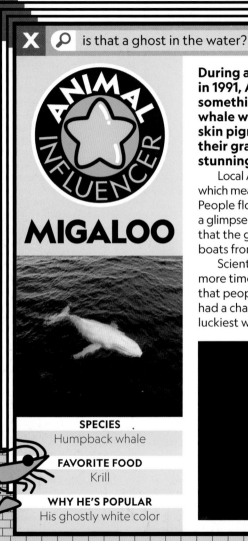

MIGALOO

During a shore-based whale survey in 1991, Australian researchers spotted something shocking: a white whale! The whale was a humpback, and it lacked the skin pigments that give most humpbacks their gray-black color. White whales are stunningly rare.

Local Aboriginal leaders named the whale Migaloo, which means "white fella." Migaloo caused a sensation. People flocked to whale-watch boats to try to catch a glimpse of the ghostly whale. He became so popular that the government made special laws to keep boats from getting too close and bothering him.

Scientists say that Migaloo will start spending more time far out to sea as he gets older. This means that people will encounter him less and less. If you've had a chance to see Migaloo, you're one of the luckiest whale-watchers in the world!

SPECIES
Humpback whale

FAVORITE FOOD
Krill

WHY HE'S POPULAR
His ghostly white color

The humpback is **NAMED FOR** the **HUMP-LIKE SHAPE** that its back makes **WHEN IT DIVES.**

Humpback whales **SOMETIMES BLOW A NET OF BUBBLES** to trap tasty fish.

Humpbacks **CAN LIVE** for **80 YEARS.** Migaloo is about 35 years old.

Dolphinstagram

dumbo_octopus
⌖ Deep ocean

SELFIE!

💜 **273 likes**

dumbo_octopus I feel cute today. To be fair, I feel cute every day. I'm a little round critter with tiny fins that I use for flap-flapping around. Too bad I live deep in the ocean, where it's too dark for you to see how cute I am. Better bring a submarine with strong lights! #FeelingCute

the nose knows

YiPadvisor

Malayan_Tapir
Snorkel Trip, Royal Belum State Park, Malaysia

Member for 2 years

I'll be honest: My snorkel trip didn't get off to a great start. I approached some humans to ask about renting equipment, and they ran away! Sure, I'm an unpredictable 650-pound (295-kg) animal with strong jaws, but—rude.

Then I remembered that my snout is a built-in snorkel! I hopped into a pond and tromped across the bottom, poking my nose up for air. I saw some cool turtles and fish. Great trip overall. I'd definitely recommend visiting (if you've got the snout).

CRITTER CHAT

RED KANGAROO

LIVES IN: Australia's deserts and grasslands
SCREEN NAME: RustyRoo

FRIENDS

SqueakyBeak
Budgerigar

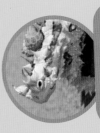

LookingSharp
Thorny devil

All_Ears
Greater bilby

...

RustyRoo

Hey pals, stay cool out there! Today's going to be a hot one. I'm glad I have a super gut that soaks up water from the plants I eat!

#AwesomeAdaptations

LookingSharp

Oh yeah? I've got special grooves in my skin that collect dew and channel it right into my mouth.

#EvenAwesomerAdaptations

SqueakyBeak

It's too early for nature facts. I'm just waking up.

All_Ears

I'm just going to bed! #ZZZ

Zz

TURN PAGE • • •

RustyRoo
Anybody want to meet up? I'm hanging out in the shade, licking my arms. (The spit carries the heat away as it dries, and I stay cool!)

SqueakyBeak
Psst, my flock's having a party at the local watering hole. Hop on by!

LookingSharp
Will there be ants? I like eating ants.

RustyRoo
You ONLY eat ants. #Obsessed

All_Ears
qpweoirupafdskkdjrrrrr

RustyRoo
Did All_Ears just post in her sleep?

SELFIE!

All_Ears
Um, ignore that last message. I'm awake now, and about to leave my burrow! Did you know that my pouch faces backward so I won't get dirt in it when I dig?
#TheAwesomestAdaptation

LookingSharp
I wish I had a pouch. I'd keep ants in there.

RustyRoo
Of COURSE you would. #StillObsessed

SqueakyBeak
Hey, keep it down! Somebudgie is trying to sleep. #ZZZ

19

CRAFTY
COMMUNICATOR

fire-flies

Imagine you're going for a walk in the park on a beautiful summer evening. Suddenly, you come across a galaxy of blinking lights. Fireflies! Your night just got a lot more special. But what, exactly, are you looking at? Why do fireflies shine at all?

"Firefly" isn't a very good name for this insect. It's not a fly—it's a beetle. And it's not on fire! The firefly's light comes from complicated chemical reactions. Also, for most of their lives, fireflies don't fly. They crawl on or under the forest floor as glowing larvae, munching on worms and other tiny soil critters. When they become fully fledged adults, it's time to find love. Male fireflies shine to attract females and scare off other males. Female fireflies answer with their own flashes.

Some fireflies shine for a more sinister reason. Female *Photuris* fireflies mimic the light shows of other types of female fireflies. When males fly in to investigate, the *Photuris* fireflies eat them. Yikes!

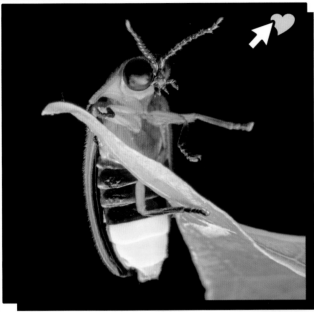

SOME KINDS of fireflies **DON'T SHINE AT ALL,** and some can't even fly.

PEOPLE TRAVEL from all over the world to the **GREAT SMOKY MOUNTAINS** to see **FIREFLIES FLASH** at the same time.

Fireflies **FLASH** in **DIFFERENT COLORS,** from orange to blue-green, **AND DIFFERENT PATTERNS,** from lines to J-shapes!

Algerian Desert
Desert_long-eared_bat

★ ★ ★ ★ ★

This place has everything I could ever want in a dining establishment! It's hot, it's dry, it's sandy, and it's packed with scorpions. My favorite meal is the deathstalker scorpion. It may be highly dangerous, but I'm mostly immune to its venom, and it's so crunchy! Yum.

Dolphinstagram

orchid_mantis
📍 Southeast Asia

261 likes

orchid_mantis Floral patterns are always in style. I look so much like a flower that other insects fly up to me, hoping to drink some sweet nectar. Then I eat them. I look so good, I literally slay. #WildStyleInspo

23

CRITTER CHAT

BOLD JUMPING SPIDER

LIVES IN: Grassy areas and sometimes homes in North America
SCREEN NAME: HairyHopper

FRIENDS

Rug_Nut
Varied carpet beetle

ShineOn
Silverfish

Max123
The family dog

HairyHopper
Hello, housemates! Are you ready to jump into a new day?

ShineOn
As a nocturnal insect, I'm ready to jump into bed.

Rug_Nut
C'mon down to the carpet, everybuggy! My beetle buds and I are hanging out, and there's plenty of dog hair for my hungry larvae. *Mmm. #PestParty*

Max123
No time to party. I can't find my humans! They went out the door and never came back!!!!! BARK BARK WHINE

ShineOn
Not this again.

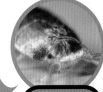

TURN PAGE

HairyHopper
I just caught a speedy fly for lunch. Glad I have eight eyes so I can follow even the fastest prey!

Max123
I wish I had some lunch! I've never eaten any food in my life!! The mail carrier just came by and I tried to eat him, but I got a mouthful of letters!!!! WHINE!!

SELFIE!

Rug_Nut
Max123, you eat twice a day. I know because my larvae eat your kibble crumbs.

Max123
LIES!!!

26

HairyHopper
What a full day of hunting and hopping. Time to crawl into a crevice to nap.

Max123
BIG NEWS! My humans came back!! And they fed me!!! BARK BARK BARK!!!

Rug_Nut
Max123, this happens every night.

Max123
Grrrrrr ...

ShineOn
Maybe we should all log off. I'm about to dive into a good book! *Mmm,* delicious books. I love eating their binding.

27

Dolphinstagram

cuviers_beaked_whale
📍 Deep-sea floor

SELFIE!

❤️ **14 likes**

cuviers_beaked_whale When I'm looking for a snack, I go deep. And I mean really deep. I drop about a mile down to the seafloor in search of tasty squid and fish. Here's me at the surface, and here's a selfie I took on my latest dive! Too bad my flash is broken.

Plains Zebra & Yellow-billed Oxpecker
● Online from a Kenyan grassland

When ticks bite my zebra pal, I'm here to help. I swoop down and eat those pests! I also drink a little zebra blood while I'm at it. OK, maybe a lot of zebra blood.
#SecretlyAVampire #BFFs

LIKE | COMMENT

29

31

CRITTER CHAT

LION

LIVES ON: Southern African savanna
SCREEN NAME: Just_Lion_Around

FRIENDS

True_Stripes
Plains zebra

RapidCat
Cheetah

NeckAndNeck
Giraffe

Just_Lion_Around
Time to *ROARRRR!*

RapidCat
Ow, my ears! What's all the fuss about?

Just_Lion_Around
Roaring is how I tell other lions that this territory is #Mine! Plus, it's fun. *ROARRR!*

RapidCat
I can't roar, so I'll have to take your word for it.

Just_Lion_Around
Really? That's sad! I'll roar twice as loud for the both of us. *ROARRRR!* This place is #Mine!

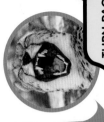

RapidCat
Sighhh.

TURN PAGE

33

Just_Lion_Around

Just a friendly reminder that this is my territory! #Mine

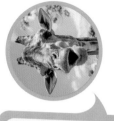

True_Stripes

We know. You won't stop posting about it. Who needs a territory? Why not just wander around like me and my herd?

NeckAndNeck

Wandering is the best. I go where the food is.

SELFIE!

Just_Lion_Around

Nah. By protecting a territory, I can take charge of a watering hole and guard the dens where the lionesses raise their cubs! It's the best. #Mine

34

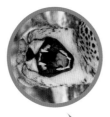

Just_Lion_Around
The sun's setting—and you know what that means!

RapidCat
Oh no. Don't tell me …

Just_Lion_Around
It's time to *ROARRRRR!*

RapidCat
Where's your territory again? I want to start avoiding it.

Just_Lion_Around
Sorry, I can't hear you over the sound of my *ROARRRRRR!*

Dolphinstagram

upside_down_jellyfish
Sandy shallows in the Caribbean Sea

 99 likes

upside_down_jellyfish Friends, are you feeling blue? Turn that frown upside down! My pals and I like to hang out on the sandy seafloor, waving our tentacles up at the sun. That sunlight feeds the algae that live in my body, and the algae make food for me. #Topsy-TurvyLife

MelodyMaker

SPECIES: House mouse

LIKES: Dark spaces, crumbs, blobs of spilled peanut butter

DISLIKES: Foxes, food sealed in tight containers

ABOUT ME: I'm looking for a female mouse who appreciates a nice melody. Like other male mice, I sing to find love. I practice all the time, and I just *know* I'll be the first mouse megastar! Some animals (like humans) can't hear my high-pitched songs. But I don't let that get me down. I know that the right house mouse won't be able to resist my squeaky serenade!

take a chance on me

connect with me!

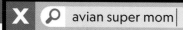

WISDOM

SPECIES
Laysan albatross

FAVORITE FOOD
Squid

WHY SHE'S POPULAR
She's the oldest
known wild bird, and
an amazing mom!

Every year, on Midway Atoll, in the middle of the Pacific Ocean, something very silly happens. Half a million gangly, long-winged seabirds called Laysan albatrosses swoop in for a landing.

They search for their lifelong partners, and once they're reunited, they dance. They clack their beaks and bob their heads. They whistle, moan, and moo. It's like the most awkward school dance ever.

The scientists who work on Midway always hope for the return of one special dancer: Wisdom. Scientists first spotted Wisdom way back in 1956, when she was about five years old. Now she's at least 70 years old—the oldest known wild bird in the world!

She's not just a survivor—she's also an amazing mom. Every year, Wisdom lays a single egg and raises a fluffy chick. So far, she has successfully reared between 30 and 36 babies. It's great news for all Laysan albatrosses, which face threats such as plastic pollution and entanglement in fishing lines. Stay wise, Wisdom!

Their **CHICKS EAT** stomach oil and squid that **THEIR PARENTS PUKE** into their mouths.

Laysan albatrosses have **SIX-FOOT** (1.8-m) **WINGSPANS.**

Laysan albatross **PARENTS** can **TRAVEL 1,600 MILES** (2,600 km) away from the nest in **SEARCH OF FOOD.**

CRITTER CHAT

AMERICAN ROBIN

LIVES IN: North American backyards
SCREEN NAME: RoundRobin

FRIENDS

TrashBandit
Raccoon

NutsAboutNuts
Gray squirrel

SongStealer
Northern mockingbird

...

RoundRobin
Just found the perfect tree for my new nest!

SELFIE!

NutsAboutNuts
Nests are the best! I'm just waking up in my nest of leaves. It's called a drey. *#HoorayForDreys*

Zz

TrashBandit
Pfft. Nests are WAY too much work. I just nap in a hollow tree.

SongStealer
Pfft. Nests are WAY too much work. I just nap in a hollow tree.

TrashBandit
Hey! Stop copying me!

TURN PAGE
• • •

43

RoundRobin
This nest is really coming together. Here's my recipe: twigs from the human's backyard, mud from the puddle in the driveway, and a soft lining of dead grass.

NutsAboutNuts
Nice! Your chicks are going to love it. *#BestMom*

SongStealer
Nice! Your chicks are going to love it. *#BestMom*

NutsAboutNuts
Seriously, stop copying us!

SongStealer
Sorry. It's what I do. I'm a mockingbird. I mock. *#DealWithIt*

RoundRobin

I'm trying to sleep. Why do I keep hearing a phone ringing?

SongStealer

I'm practicing mimicking different noises! Ring ring ring ring! BEEP BEEP BEEP!

TrashBandit

Shh! I'm raiding the trash can, and you'll wake up the humans.

SongStealer

Shh! I'm raiding the trash can, and you'll wake up the humans.

TrashBandit

Argh. You're being a real birdbrain.

CRAFTY
COMMUNICATOR

orcas

"Hi, y'all!" "G'day, mate!" "Top of the mornin' to ya!" If you've got friends from other parts of the world, you may notice that they sound different. They may have accents or use unfamiliar words. In the 1980s, orca scientists noticed something amazing: Groups of orcas also make their own unique sounds!

Orcas live in noisy family groups called pods. These dolphins whistle, squeak, trill, and screech, and each pod does it in a unique way. Researchers listening in on their calls can easily tell the groups apart. Just as human accents from the same parts of the country tend to be similar, pods that hang out together sound more alike.

What are these noisy orcas saying? We don't know. They tend to be chattier when they're looking for food. Maybe it's like you and your friends talking at lunch, sharing jokes and news—but with more fresh salmon and less PB&J.

SOME orcas **HUNT** the largest animals on the planet: **BLUE WHALES!**

You can easily tell male and female orcas apart. **MALES** have **EXTRA TALL DORSAL** (back) **FINS.**

Orcas **CAN LIVE** for **80 YEARS OR MORE.**

48

Dolphinstagram

virginia_opossum
📍 North America

 26 likes

virginia_opossum Motherhood is wonderful, but the responsibility really weighs on me sometimes. That's because I'm carrying seven babies on my back! They're too big for my pouch now, so they get a free piggyback ride. **#MomLife**

Dolphinstagram

goblin_shark
◆Deep-sea floor

SELFIE!

♥ **103 likes**

goblin_shark A random octopus told me to smile more. So, I did. I guess he didn't know that I can stick my jaw out three inches (8 cm) from my mouth! He jetted away really fast. Too bad—he looked tasty. #BeCarefulWhatYouWishFor

where
am i??

YiPadvisor

Arctic_tern
Madagascar

Madagascar is fine. The lemurs are nice. The baobab trees are impressively tall. The local seafood is delicious. There's just one problem. I DIDN'T MEAN TO WIND UP IN MADAGASCAR!

I must have gotten blown off course. This is so embarrassing. I hope one of the lemur locals can point me in the right direction ...

Member for
2 years

CRITTER CHAT

GREAT WHITE SHARK

LIVES IN: The open ocean
SCREEN NAME: JustJawesome

FRIENDS

MobyClick
Sperm whale

Water_Wings
Green sea turtle

SealTheDeal
Northern elephant seal

JustJawesome
Time to sink all 300 of my teeth into a bright new day.

MobyClick
That's quite the mouth! I only have a couple dozen teeth, and they're only on my bottom jaw.

JustJawesome
Why so few chompers? Don't you eat meat?

MobyClick
I don't need teeth to slurp up nice soft squid!

JustJawesome
Mmm. I could go for some calamari.

TURN PAGE

SELFIE!

JustJawesome
I wave my big tail back and forth as I cruise the open sea. What's your swimming style?

MobyClick
I flap my tail flukes up and down. #DifferentStrokes

Water_Wings
I fly through the water using my big front flippers! #WaterWings

SealTheDeal
I use my back flippers to power me forward, and my front ones to steer. I'm speedy in the water. Elephant seal? More like cheetah seal!

JustJawesome

I just jumped out of the water and got a look at the world above the surface! I think I might have seen an arctic tern fly by? Anyway, it sure is pretty up there.

SealTheDeal

It is! Did you know that I leave the ocean every year to give birth? Beaches are beautiful.

Water_Wings

I lay my eggs on beaches, too.

JustJawesome

I wish I could hit the beach. Every time I get close to shore, humans look at me funny. Maybe they're jealous of my amazing smile!

BEAST | FRIENDS | FUREVER

Arctic Fox & Polar Bear
● Online from the Arctic

It can be hard to find a meal during the icy Arctic winter. So, I follow in the footsteps of my polar bear BFF. When he kills a tasty seal, I chomp on the leftover scraps. I love our friendship so much that it makes me blubber! **#BFFs**

LIKE | COMMENT

 **Dolphinstagram**

honduran_white_bat
Central American forest

 914 likes

honduran_white_bat Camping is so much fun! My pals and I make our own tent by nipping the veins of a big leaf until it droops down over us. We cozy up together and tell ghost stories. Who wants to hear the one about the ghostly bat with a hook for a wing? oooOOOOoooOOOoooo

Dead Horse Arum Lily
Blowfly

★☆☆☆☆

If you're like me, you love feasting on the smelly carcass of a dead animal. That's why you should AVOID this flower. Its fleshy color and putrid smell are enough to entice any insect. Fly in close, though, and you won't find any rotting meat. In fact, this plant will just trick you into spreading its pollen. The whole thing stinks (in a bad way).

yowl

hard pass!

59

 **llamazon**
the **BEAST** place to shop

 for aspiring tough guy

Manly Man Silver Hair Dye

MANLY MAN SILVER HAIR DYE

young gorilla approved!

CUSTOMER REVIEWS

★ ★ ★ ★ ★ **Color me happy!!!!**

Mountain_gorilla Verified Customer

I'm a young male gorilla, so I'm not a silver-back yet. When I'm older, my back fur will turn silver gray. But why wait? This dye will fool any ape, so long as they don't look too closely! My chest pounding is now 85 percent more intimidating, and my mom says I look tough.

Dolphinstagram

northern_pudu
📍 The Andes mountain range

❤️ **650 likes**

northern_pudu Everybody fawns over me because I'm the tiniest deer in the world. How tiny? When I grow up, I'll be just about 14 inches (36 cm) tall at the shoulder. Hold up two pencils end to end—I'm shorter than that! As deer go, I'm the dearest. #FeelingCute

CRITTER CHAT

NAKED MOLE RAT WORKER

LIVES IN: Dry tropical grassland in Ethiopia
SCREEN NAME: Digging_It

FRIENDS

Her_Royal_Highness
Naked mole rat queen

WartsAndAll
Common warthog

LeggyLeaper
Serval

Digging_It
Good morning! Not that the time of day matters much to me. I'm always digging and fixing up the colony's tunnel system. Anything for my queen!

LeggyLeaper
What? You have a queen??

Her_Royal_Highness
Like an ant colony, a naked mole rat colony exists to serve its queen. As queen, I give birth to the workers.

Digging_It
Well said, Your Majesty!

Her_Royal_Highness
Get back to digging.

Digging_It
Yes, Your Majesty!

TURN PAGE

63

Digging_It
Dig dig dig. This burrow's turning out great. *#SoilSelfie*

WartsAndAll
Looking good! All that digging sounds like a lot of work. I just live in an old aardvark burrow. It's cozy!

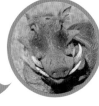

LeggyLeaper
I do love napping in a nice aardvark burrow, even if it smells a little aardvarky.

Digging_It
My queen smells wonderful.

Her_Royal_Majesty
Thank you. Now keep digging.

Digging_It
Whew! I finished my tunnel. I hope my 72 colony-mates will approve.

WartsAndAll
Yikes—that's a big colony. My family group is only about 10 hogs strong.

LeggyLeaper
That's still too many critters! I live alone. I need my personal space.

Her_Royal_Highness
Good job with the tunnel, Digging_It. Now take a quick nap and dig me another tunnel.

Digging_It
Yes, Your Majesty!

Dolphinstagram

greater_rhea
📍 South American grasslands

 71 likes

greater_rhea Unlike many other male birds, I'm in charge of incubating eggs. I'm a proud papa—and a fierce nest protector. Don't bother my nest or you'll be in rheal trouble! #DadLife

bharmony

SealedWithLove

SPECIES: Hooded seal
LIKES: Fish, shrimp, cold swims on cold mornings
DISLIKES: Orcas, melting ice caps

ABOUT ME: I don't need a male seal with a fancy car. I don't care if he can cook. I don't need to hear any fancy poetry. There's just one thing I want to know: Does he have a bright pink balloon on his face? If a male hooded seal inflates his fleshy pink nose balloon, I know he's trying to show me that he's big and strong. So don't bring me a rose—just blow up your nose!

You matched!
with ROSYNOSY

color me
intrigued

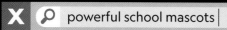

RALPHIE

Plenty of colleges have mascots, but there's one mascot that can literally crush the competition. Meet Ralphie, the 1,200-pound (540-kg) mascot of the University of Colorado Buffaloes.

In 1934, the university's newspaper ran a contest to pick an animal to be the school's mascot, and the buffalo was chosen. Some students rented a young buffalo and brought it to the football team's final game of the season. The team won seven to zero! So was the buffalo good luck? Just in case, students kept bringing buffalo to games. In 1966, someone gave the university its own buffalo, and since then, other buffalo have followed. (Nobody's exactly sure why she's named Ralphie.)

American buffalo, aka bison, are the largest land animals in North America. Ralphie has 15 human handlers who take care of her, and when she goes to games, five of them walk alongside her to keep her safe. The school chose a female bison because males are even larger—they can weigh more than 2,000 pounds (900 kg)!

SPECIES
American bison

FAVORITE FOOD
Hay and other plants

WHY SHE'S POPULAR
She's a good luck charm for football players!

BABY BISON are called **"RED DOGS"** because they're pale reddish brown.

When an American bison **GETS MAD,** it sticks its **TAIL STRAIGHT UP.**

Their sharp **HORNS** can **GROW** to **OVER TWO FEET** (0.6 m) **LONG!**

CRITTER CHAT

BAIRD'S TAPIR

LIVES IN: Cloud forest of Monteverde, Costa Rica
SCREEN NAME: WhoNose

FRIENDS

Hoot_And_Holler
Mantled howler monkey

JungleJewel
Resplendent quetzal

EyesInTheSkies
Forest giant owl butterfly

WhoNose

Another damp day in the cloud forest! That's how I like it. The clouds' moisture keeps the vegetation well watered, lush, and DELICIOUS.

JungleJewel

I love it, too! All that greenery matches my glorious plumage. #FeelingCute

Hoot_And_Holler

Hey WhoNose, have you tried eating tree leaves? Tasty! You should climb up into my tree and eat some.

WhoNose

I weigh 600 pounds (272 kg). #NotGonnaHappen

TURN PAGE ● ● ●

71

5:48 a.m.

WhoNose
OK, which one of you woke me up from my nap with that horrible sound?

EyesInTheSkies
Not me. Butterflies aren't very noisy.

JungleJewel
Did it sound like chirps?

WhoNose
More like nightmarish screeching howls.

Hoot_And_Holler
Um. Guilty.

SELFIE!

72

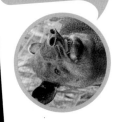

WhoNose

Watch out, friends! I just saw a hungry puma! Luckily, I'm the biggest land animal in the forest, so I'm not an easy meal.

EyesInTheSkies

If it comes near me, I'll flash the scary eye spots on my wings!

JungleJewel

I'll fly away! And Hoot_And_Holler can scare it with horrible howls.

Hoot_And_Holler

Oh NOW you like my howls. Plug your ears, pals. It's about to get LOUD.

Dolphinstagram

clouded_leopard
📍 Southeast Asia

 127 likes

clouded_leopard Some might say that leopard print is passé, but don't let them cloud your judgment. You've never seen spots like mine. I'm a tree climber, and my cloudy spots help me hide among branches and leaves. The forest is my catwalk! #WildStyleInspo

bharmony

MusicalMoth

SPECIES: Yellow peach moth
LIKES: Peach, macadamia, and durian trees
DISLIKES: Rainstorms, hungry birds

ABOUT ME: A lot of people look at me and think, "He's just a moth. He can't possibly make music!" But they're wrong. To impress females and scare away rival males, I vibrate a membrane in my abdomen that makes a rattling noise. It's not exactly a symphony, but if you're looking for a strange new sound, I'm your moth!

let's harmonize

connect with me!

75

CRAFTY
COMMUNICATOR

black-capped chickadees

If you live in the northern United States or southern Canada, you might see black-capped chickadees at your backyard feeder. These cute birds chatter back and forth to each other with a sound like *chick-a-dee!* Believe it or not, the chirps are a secret code that helps chickadees warn each other about danger.

Plenty of predators, from hawks to owls to raccoons, want to make a snack out of a chickadee. When a chickadee spots a predator, it calls out *chick-a-dee* to warn its flock mates of danger. The more dangerous the threat, the more *dee*'s it adds to the end of its *chick-a-dee* call! A truly dangerous predator might get 23 *dee*'s. That's *chick-a-dee-dee-dee-dee-dee-dee-dee-dee-dee-dee-dee-dee-dee-dee-dee-dee-dee-dee-dee-dee-dee-dee*. Yikes.

Chickadees make lots of other calls, including a two-note song that says, "This is my tree!" All told, they produce at least 16 sounds. Next time they come to your bird feeder, listen close and *chick* them out!

Black-capped chickadees **HIDE FOOD FOR LATER.** They can remember thousands of hiding places.

Chickadees build their **NESTS INSIDE HOLES IN TREES.**

Dolphinstagram

whale_shark
📍 Warm oceans around the world

 42 likes

whale_shark Check out my supercool spots and stripes! Every whale shark has its own unique pattern, sort of like a human fingerprint. My streaky sides are special—and snazzy.
#WildStyleInspo

CRITTER CHAT

RING-TAILED LEMUR

LIVES IN: Forests and open areas in Madagascar
SCREEN NAME: PutARingOnIt

FRIENDS

Petite_Primate
Madame Berthe's mouse lemur

FreakyFingers
Aye-aye

LargeLemur
Indri

PutARingOnIt
WOW! I just found out that there aren't any wild lemurs outside Madagascar! Isn't that ... wild?

LargeLemur
No way! The rest of the world is missing out. We're really great.

Petite_Primate
Yes, and we come in such a wonderful mix of shapes and sizes! Huge ones like LargeLemur, stripy-tailed ones like PutARingOnIt, teensy ones like me ... and then there are the weirdos.

FreakyFingers
You rang?

SELFIE!

Petite_Primate
LOL

TURN PAGE

PutARingOnIt
My troop is on the move! Keep an ear out! We wail and moan to keep in touch.

Petite_Primate
Ugh. Keep it down! Not all lemurs are active during the day. #BeautySleep

LargeLemur
My mate and I were just about to start a wailing duet. Whoop! Whoop!

Petite_Primate
Forget what I said about lemur diversity. I wish there were fewer of us.

PutARingOnIt
Don't joke. Many of us are endangered.

82

PutARingOnIt
What a good day! I ate 11 tamarind fruits and spread my scent on 24 trees. Bedtime for me— and a warm welcome to the lemur night shift!

FreakyFingers
Thank you! Time to get tapping!

PutARingOnIt
Tapping?

FreakyFingers
When I hunt, I tap my long finger on a tree and listen for grubs.

PutARingOnIt
You're one peculiar primate.

FreakyFingers
Aye sure am!

Scarlet_macaw
Chuncho Macaw Clay Lick

⭐ ⭐ ⭐ ⭐ ⭐

Hey you! Hit the dirt!

Member for
4 years

Seriously. If you want to be a healthy parrot in the Amazon rainforest, you should find some dirt. Clay soil is packed with minerals that healthy birds need, and the dirt at Chuncho Macaw Clay Lick is some of the tastiest. My macaw friends and I gather here to squawk, play, and chomp on clay. And we're not the only ones. A rainbow of parrot species flock to the area, from huge red-and-green macaws to smaller mealy amazons to teeny parakeets. It's a dirty delight.

yowl

never again!

Whistling Thorn Tree

Giraffe

★☆☆☆☆

When I first saw this tree, I thought its leaves looked tasty. I stretched my neck, opened my mouth, stuck out my long tongue, and ... OW! An ant bit me! This tree grows special "rooms" for ants to live in. The ants get a home, and they protect the tree from harm. I don't like it when my meal bites back!

Dolphinstagram

turkey_vulture
📍 North and South America

💜 **420 likes**

turkey_vulture I look so cute today! Doesn't my bare head look adorably rosy? And my feathers are golden brown in the sunlight. I can't wait to show off my look to the other vultures when we meet up later at the stinky deer carcass by the side of the highway!
#FeelingCute

CRITTER CHAT

GRIZZLY BEAR

LIVES IN: Yellowstone National Park
SCREEN NAME: Grizz_Kid

FRIENDS

Howl_n_Prowl
Gray wolf

FancyAntlers
Elk

YouHerdMe
American bison

Grizz_Kid

Hey, did y'all know that we live in the oldest national park in the United States?

FancyAntlers

What's a national park again?

Grizz_Kid

It's a place that preserves nature and lets people explore it.

FancyAntlers

Oh, THAT's why there are always so many humans trying to take pictures of me! Good thing I grew an extra handsome pair of antlers this year. #PrettyProngs

TURN PAGE

Grizz_Kid

Yikes. A human just got WAY too close to me. Don't people know that I'm a dangerous animal??

YouHerdMe

The same thing happened to me. I was napping—then suddenly I was surrounded by humans snapping pictures. They woke me up! #PeskyPeople

Howl_n_Prowl

Tell me about it! My pack was trying to sneak up on you at the exact same time. So much for a bison breakfast. #PeskyPeople

YouHerdMe

Yeah! Wait... HEY.

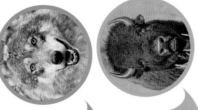

5:39 p.m.

Grizz_Kid
See, now THAT photographer is being respectful. She's sitting in a car, using a long lens to quietly take pictures from a distance.

Howl_n_Prowl
I bet she takes great photos, too.

YouHerdMe
You should ask to see the pics!

FancyAntlers
Yeah, do it!

Grizz_Kid
I would, but I know she got some pictures of me yawning … and burping. #EmBearassed

93

CRAFTY COMMUNICATOR

white rhino

Imagine if you were walking down the street and you stumbled across a steaming pile of poo. You'd probably pinch your nose and back away. But if you were a white rhinoceros, a pile of dung would be an exciting find—and you'd jam your nose right into it!

Groups of white rhinos poop in the same spot, making a pile some 65 feet (20 m) across. That's more than the length of a city bus. The dung is packed with chemicals, and by sniffing it, rhinos can learn about each other's age, health, territory, and more. It's a gentle, if gross, way to chat.

If a male rhino sniffs poop and learns that there's another male around, he can avoid a fight. That's important for a species with two sharp spikes on its face!

White rhinos aren't the only animals that communicate with poo. Hippos, gazelles, rabbits, monkeys, and all sorts of other animals do it, too. Next time you go for a nature hike, be careful not to step in a conversation.

Their **POOP** actually **DOESN'T SMELL** too bad! It's **MOSTLY** made of dried **GRASS.**

The **ONLY** land animals **BIGGER** than white rhinos are African and Asian **ELEPHANTS.**

On **HOT DAYS,** white rhinos **LOVE** to wallow in **MUD.**

#bffs

:paw_prints: BEAST | :heart: FRIENDS | ∞ FUREVER

Warthog & Banded Mongoose
● Online from sub-Saharan Africa

Sometimes I'm itching for company. Sometimes I'm itching because I'm covered in ticks and bugs. My mongoose BFF hangs out with me and nips pests off my skin. Hey buddy, let's sTICK together!
#BFFs

| LIKE | COMMENT |

Dolphinstagram

japanese_dwarf_flying_squirrel
📍 Honshu and Kyushu islands, Japan

 1,012 likes

japanese_dwarf_flying_squirrel Huge eyes? Check. Round body? Check. Fluffy tail, pink nose, tiny paws? Check, check, check! Just wait until I leap into the air and glide using the skin that stretches between my ankles and wrists. That's when I really look fly. #FeelingCute

CRITTER CHAT

GIANT GREEN ANEMONE

LIVES IN: The intertidal zone in California, U.S.A.
SCREEN NAME: Shore_Thing

FRIENDS

WellShelled
Black turban snail

TideRider
Tidepool sculpin

RockStar
Bat star

Shore_Thing
I'm thinking of catching some prey with my stinging tentacles, but I'm not sure what to fish for. What are y'all eating for breakfast?

WellShelled
I'm slurping up algae! *#EatYourGreens*

TideRider
I'm chomping on barnacles! *#BarnacleBrunch*

RockStar
I love barnacles. When I find one, I stretch my stomach over it. My digestive juices dissolve it into a slurry, and I slurp up the goo. Yum.

Shore_Thing
I'm not hungry anymore.

TURN PAGE
• • •

Shore_Thing
Problem solved: I remembered that I have a built-in snack machine. Green algae live in my body and feed me extra nutrients!

TideRider
Wow, that's like a superpower! Want to know my superpower? I can change color to match my surroundings.

WellShelled
I move really, really slowly. Is that a superpower?

TideRider
Only if you're trying to bore your enemies to death.

Shore_Thing
The tide sure is high now, and these waves are strong! Good thing I have a special plate that keeps me stuck to the rocks.

RockStar
My sucker-covered feet anchor me so I don't wash away.

TideRider
Why not go with the flow? I swim all over during high tide. I'll find my way home with my amazing sense of smell.

RockStar
Wow! What do I smell like?

TideRider
Barnacle juice.

103

Dolphinstagram

timber_rattlesnake
📍 Eastern United States

 800 likes

timber_rattlesnake I have a fierce reputation, but I'm here to rattle your assumptions! I'm a kind, caring mom. I protect my babies, keep them warm, and stop them from slithering into danger. #MomLife

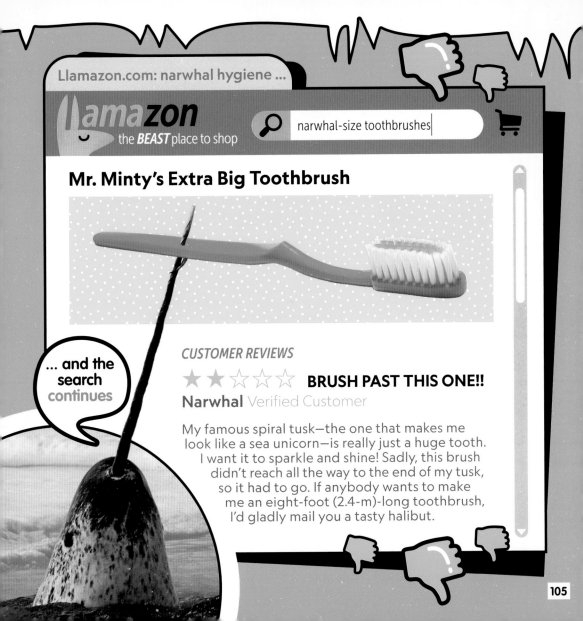

ANIMAL INFLUENCER

BRIGADIER SIR
NILS
OLAV

If you visit Scotland's Edinburgh Zoo, you'll find the largest outdoor penguin pool in Europe. It's full of penguins of all kinds, but one bird is a cut above the rest. He's Brigadier Sir Nils Olav, the penguin knight!

Is he a real knight? And more important, does he ride a tiny horse? Sadly, the answer to both of these questions is no. In 1961, Lieutenant Nils Egelien of the Norwegian King's Guard visited the Edinburgh Zoo and fell head over heels for the penguins. When the guards came back to the zoo in 1972, they symbolically adopted a penguin and gave him a name that's a combo of Lieutenant Nils and Norway's King Olav V.

Each time the King's Guard visits, they give the penguin a "promotion." There's even a bronze statue of Sir Nils Olav outside the penguin pool. All this fame hasn't gone to his head. He still swims and squawks and eats fish alongside his lower-ranking companions.

SPECIES
King penguin

FAVORITE FOOD
Fish

WHY HE'S POPULAR
He's the only penguin that's also a knight.

Rather than building nests, they **INCUBATE** their **EGGS ON THEIR FEET!**

King penguins are the **SECOND LARGEST PENGUINS,** after emperor penguins.

FEMALE king penguins **LAY JUST ONE EGG** during each nesting **SEASON.**

yow!

highly recommend!

Volcano near Mexico City
Volcano_rabbit

★★★★★

For most folks, a volcano may not sound like a safe place to live. But for me, this place is exploding with possibilities. In the wet season, the ground just erupts with tasty grasses! What more could you ask for? I lava good volcano.

bharmony

PackMate

SPECIES: Gray wolf
LIKES: Howling, eating deer
DISLIKES: Fast deer

ABOUT ME: I'm looking for a male who can help me start a pack. He must be good at hunting moose, defending a territory of 50 square miles (130 sq km), and barfing up meat to feed our pups. If you've got the moose-hunting, territory-guarding, meat-puking skills I need, give me a howl!

109

CRITTER CHAT

9:20 a.m.

JustJawesome
I just saw a terrible movie about a great white shark that eats humans. It made sharks seem so dangerous!

MobyClick
Ugh. I feel you. One of the most famous human books is about a violent sperm whale. As if! #SoWrong

JustJawesome
Ridiculous! Humans are WAY more of a threat to us than we are to them.

JustJawesome

Mmm. That was some tasty tuna. Anyway, here's why humans are wrong: Sharks don't like eating them! Sometimes I accidentally bite one, but I usually spit it out. *#yuck*

Water_Wings

Oh no!

JustJawesome

Meanwhile, humans catch sharks in nets, either on purpose—or by accident, when they're looking for other fish.

Water_Wings

Argh. Well, I have my own frustrations with humans. They put plastic in the sea and I eat it, thinking it's jellyfish. *#yuck*

TURN PAGE
● ● ●

111

JustJawesome
I'm still thinking about that awful shark movie.

SealTheDeal
You should write a critical review of it and post it online!

JustJawesome
Yeah! I think I will! I'm going to give it zero stars and say, "This movie bites ... but in a bad way."

SealTheDeal
Nice one.

Dolphinstagram

leopard_gecko
📍 South Asian deserts

❤️ **420 likes**

leopard_gecko My tail is fat and fabulous. It's also a survival pack. When I've got plenty to eat, I store energy as fat in my tail. When the pickings are slim, I turn that fat into energy so I can stay alive. Big tail, can't fail! #Tailfie

CRAFTY
COMMUNICATOR

poison frogs

If you wore a flashy, bright-colored outfit to a party, you'd want your friends to come up and say, "You look great!" But poison frogs use their colors to send a totally different message: "LEAVE ME ALONE."

Poison frogs live in tropical Central and South America. They're very cute, with puppy-dog eyes and mouths curled up into little smiles. You may be tempted to give them a hug—but don't do it! Dangerous toxins ooze through their skin. A single golden poison frog can kill 10 people. A hungry bird or other predator just needs to take one little nip of a poison frog before it learns a painful lesson: Avoid any brightly colored amphibian!

That's why poison frogs can hop around during the day, right out in the open. Their fashion-forward hues are a warning, keeping them stylish AND safe.

There are many **TYPES** of poison frogs, but **ONLY A HANDFUL** are poisonous enough to be **DEADLY TO HUMANS.**

POISON FROGS come in a **RAINBOW OF COLORS,** from mint green to neon yellow to deep blue.

Poison frog **DADS CARRY** their **TADPOLES** on their **BACKS.**

Dolphinstagram

graceful_decorator_crab
📍 Northern Pacific Ocean

❤️ **48 likes**

graceful_decorator_crab The ocean is my style! I have little hooks on my back that I use to "wear" any pretty algae, sponges, and other critters I find. My decorations keep me classy—and camouflaged from hungry predators. Fashion AND function? Count me in! #WildStyleInspo

don't take me back!

YiPadvisor

Mule_deer
Migration Through Western Wyoming
🐾 🐾 🐾 🐾 🐾

Member for
2 years

My friends and I just migrated from our summer range in the mountains to our winter range in the Red Desert—about 150 miles (240 km). We had fun at first. We even saw a lost arctic tern fly by! But then we ran out of stuff to talk about.

We tried playing I Spy, but the answer was always "grass." We tried naming things that started with all the letters of the alphabet, but we got bored after antler and buck. We tried having a sing-along, but none of us listen to the radio. Migration? More like sigh-gration.

Dolphinstagram

snow_leopard
📍 The Himalaya

SELFIE!

 57 likes

snow_leopard My tail is the ultimate accessory. It helps me balance as I climb steep mountains. Also, I can wrap it around me like the biggest, warmest scarf. My tail helps me stay warm—and look cool! #Tailfie

CRITTER CHAT

SPOTTED SALAMANDER

LIVES IN: The soil under temperate North American forests

SCREEN NAME: SoftSpot

FRIENDS

GalaxyNose
Star-nosed mole

Smooth_Noodle
Smooth earth snake

WiggleRoom
Common earthworm

SoftSpot
Pee-ew. My burrow is stinky today. Time to tidy it up.

GalaxyNose
Why not dig yourself a new burrow?

SoftSpot
Spotted salamanders can't dig. We just live in abandoned mammal burrows. This one still smells like chipmunk!

WiggleRoom
Just eat dirt.

SoftSpot
What?? RUDE!

WiggleRoom
No, really! That's how I burrow: I crawl along and eat my way through the soil, pooping it out as I go.

TURN PAGE ● ● ●

SoftSpot

Just heard some humans tromping by overhead, ooh-ing and aah-ing about the beauty of the forest. But the underground world is just as cool, even if they can't see it!

SELFIE!

GalaxyNose

Right? My star-shaped nose is one of the world's hidden wonders! I use it to feel my way through the darkness.

Smooth_Noodle

Oh, yeah? I have a cool ability, too: I poop when I'm threatened.

SoftSpot

Why is everything about poop today??

124

9:00 p.m.

SoftSpot
Mmm, time for a late-night snack. What should I eat? I'm thinking spiders or centipedes.

Smooth_Noodle
I always like a good earthworm.

GalaxyNose
Same here. I can chomp one down in seconds.

WiggleRoom
Y'all, I'm RIGHT HERE.

SoftSpot
Where? Text me your location!

WiggleRoom
Um, never mind ...

Dolphinstagram

atlantic_spotted_dolphin
📍 Tropical Atlantic Ocean

💜 **11 likes**

atlantic_spotted_dolphin Would you believe that when I was little, I had no spots at all? I started getting spotty when I was about three. Look at me now! I'm a spectacular speckled senior citizen of the seas.

bharmony

i wanna dance with somebody

SparkleButt

SPECIES: Peacock spider
LIKES: Crickets, hanging out on the forest floor
DISLIKES: Dance clubs that won't let spiders in

ABOUT ME: If you're looking for a dance partner, search no further! I've got a rainbow-colored backside and the right steps to show it off. I flail my legs! I tap on a twig! I sway back and forth! My moves will amaze you. Just one request: Don't be a hater. Some females will eat a male for lunch if they don't like his groove. I'd rather live to dance another day.

connect with me!

127

Common Milkweed Plant
Monarch_caterpillar
★ ★ ★ ★ ★

This milkweed is the tastiest plant in the world! Plus, I love its big floppy leaves and beautiful pink flowers. Hmm, maybe I'm a teensy bit biased. It's the only plant a monarch caterpillar is able to eat. Still, five stars!

129

Dolphinstagram

brilliant-thighed_poison_frog
📍 Amazon rainforest

💙 **88 likes**

brilliant-thighed_poison_frog Just another dad day taking care of my tadpoles. I guard my babies from predators and carry them to pools where they can swim. I love keeping my kids healthy and hoppy. #DadLife

too risky!!

Live_sharksucker_remora
Ocean Cruise on a Lemon Shark
🐾 🐾 🐾 🐾 🐾

Member for
2 years

Like all remoras, I travel in style. There's a suction cup on my head that helps me stick to whales, sharks, boats, and more. I relax while my host carries me to new and exciting places! What reMOREa could I want?

Recently I decided to take an ocean cruise on a lemon shark. At first, I was having tons of fun. My shark ate a lot of prey, so I got to feed on plenty of leftover scraps. Usually sharks leave me alone to do my thing, but this time another lemon shark tried to eat me! Next time I'll stick to a laid-back old sea turtle instead.

131

GIANT PANDA

LIVES IN: China's cool
mountain bamboo forests
SCREEN NAME: BambooBear

CRITTER CHAT

FRIENDS

Phancy_Pheasant
Golden pheasant

NoNose
Golden snub-
nosed monkey

TakinMyTime
Golden takin

...

BambooBear
On my schedule for today: eating bamboo for 12 straight hours. I won't stop until I've munched 28 pounds (13 kg) of it.

NoNose
Wow. That's how much I weigh!

BambooBear
Bamboo isn't very nutritious, so I have to eat a lot of it. I poop all day.

Phancy_Pheasant
Fun fact—bamboo is just a giant grass. You're more of a grazing cow than a bear!

BambooBear
Grr. Come say that to my sharp canine teeth.

TURN PAGE
• • •

BambooBear
As usual, I'm not feeling very social today. Good thing I can smell if there are other pandas nearby! (And avoid them.) *#MyNoseKnows*

TakinMyTime
Nice. My huge schnoz helps warm up the freezing mountain air before I breathe it in. *#HonkerHeat*

NoNose
Enough nose talk! I'm sensitive about my tiny snout.

Phancy_Pheasant
Aww. Take it from a 1.2 pound (0.5 kg) bird: Small can be beautiful.

BambooBear
BIG NEWS: I just heard that protecting panda habitat helps conserve all sorts of other critters. You should all thank me for being so cute!

TakinMyTime
Thanks, BambooBear! But no thanks for pooping all over the landscape.

Phancy_Pheasant
Yup. Giant panda, giant poops.

NoNose
Now I wish my nose were even smaller ...

Dolphinstagram

flamboyant_cuttlefish
📍 Australian coast

💜 **348 likes**

flamboyant_cuttlefish Some days I just can't decide on a style. Good thing I can change my color and texture instantly. Do I want to be white or purple? Smooth or bumpy? Anything goes! I keep the fashion world on its toes—and tentacles. #WildStyleInspo

bharmony

AmorousAmphibian

SPECIES: Eastern spadefoot toad
LIKES: Juicy caterpillars, juicy beetles, juicy earthworms
DISLIKES: Hungry snakes

ABOUT ME: I spend most of my time hanging out underground, but on warm rainy nights I burst to the surface and sing a love song like no other. Would you like to read a sample of my lyrics? Here you go:

WAAAAAAAAA

Toadally amazing, right? If you want to hear more, come to the rain-filled pool by the old pine tree. Until then, I'll leave you with these final words of love:

WAAAAAAAAA

WAAAAAAAAA

looking for a lady with melody

connect with me!

137

yowl

comfort
first!

My Shell
Pancake_tortoise

★ ★ ★ ★ ★

My shell is the place to be! It's flat and flexible like a pancake, so I can squeeze into any narrow rock crevice to hide. You'll have to take my word for it, though, since my shell is part of my body, and I can't crawl out of it. Don't be shellous!

Magnificent Sea Anemone & Common Clownfish
● Online from Northwest Australia

My anemone BFF and I work so well together. I chase away fish that want to eat her, and she lets me hide in her stinging tentacles so I stay safe from predators. Without my anemone friend, life would be pretty dark—because I'd be inside some hungry fish's stomach!
#BFFs

LIKE   COMMENT

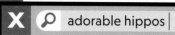

FIONA

Fiona the hippo is a superstar. People come from all over the world to visit her at her home in the Cincinnati Zoo. They love her floppy ears, her big brown eyes, and the way she splashes and plays in her 70,000-gallon (265,000-L) pool. But they especially love that she's one tough hippo.

Fiona was born in January 2017—six weeks premature. She was tiny, weak, and unable to stand. Vets didn't know if she would survive. But as she got around-the-clock care, she *slowwwwly* gained weight and learned to walk. She even started splashing around in her kiddie pool.

These days, you can visit the zoo and see Fiona diving, playing, and napping with her mom, Bibi. Though she weighed just 29 pounds (13 kg) at birth, she's plumping up fast. All grown up, she weighs about 3,000 pounds (1,400 kg). You grow, girl!

SPECIES
Common hippopotamus

FAVORITE FOOD
Grain and hay

WHY SHE'S POPULAR
She's cute—
and a survivor!

When a hippo **DIVES,** its **NOSTRILS CLOSE** so that it doesn't get water up its nose.

Their closest living **RELATIVES** are **WHALES** and **DOLPHINS.**

Though they love the water, **HIPPOS CAN'T SWIM— THEY WALK** along the bottom.

Dolphinstagram

jorunna_parva
📍 Pacific Ocean

❤️ **420 likes**

jorunna_parva *Shh.* This fuzzy bunny has a secret. I'm actually a sea slug, and my "ears" help me sniff out chemicals in the water around me. I may be more slimy than soft, but I still think I'm the cutest slug in the sea! #FeelingCute

CRITTER CHAT

GIANT TUBE WORM

LIVES IN: Hydrothermal vents in the eastern Pacific Ocean

SCREEN NAME: ReadMyLips

FRIENDS

DeepSeaShell
Giant clam

Claws_And_Effect
Hydrothermal vent crab

FishTail
Rattail fish

ReadMyLips

Sigh. I can't tell if I look cute today because it's pitch black down here. Also, I don't have eyes.

Claws_And_Effect

Deep-sea life has its drawbacks. But you're a seven-foot (2-m)-tall worm with gigantic red "lips," so I'm sure you look gorgeous.

ReadMyLips

Aww! That makes me feel warm inside.

FishTail

I also feel warm, but mostly because of the magma-heated water from this hydrothermal vent.

ReadMyLips

That too.

TURN PAGE

ReadMyLips
Does anyone else keep hearing about this thing called the "sun"? It's supposed to be brilliant!

DeepSeaShell
I heard it helps a food called "plants" grow. But who needs plants? Bacteria in my body make food for me from chemicals that seep from the vents.

ReadMyLips
I get my food from bacteria, too!

FishTail
And I've got plenty of tiny critters and scraps to eat.

ReadMyLips
Right. This "sun" doesn't sound like a very bright idea to me.

ReadMyLips
Do you ever feel stressed out?
Like you're under a lot of pressure?

FishTail
We all feel the pressure. That's because there's
a mile and a half of water pressing down on us.

DeepSeaShell
We live in an extreme place, but I think
it makes us extra tough and unique.

ReadMyLips
That's pretty deep! Get it? Deep?

DeepSeaShell
Ughhhh

149

Dolphinstagram

rainbow_agama
◉ Sub-Saharan Africa

♥ **84 likes**

rainbow_agama Why pick one hue when there's a whole rainbow of options? I love my oranges, blues, purples, pinks, and greens. I can even change my colors to match my mood! If that doesn't impress you, I'll do push-ups to show off. *#WildStyleInspo*

WaterWalker

SPECIES: Western grebe
LIKES: Pristine lakes, tasty fish
DISLIKES: Motorboats, being misidentified as a duck

ABOUT ME: I won't dance around it—I need a partner who's got moves. We western grebes are famous for our fancy footwork. Can you bob, preen, and arch your neck? That's great, but it's not enough. Can you launch yourself out of the water and run 66 feet (20 m) across the surface? If so, let's dance!

You matched! with DANCINGREBE

CRAFTY COMMUNICATOR

coyotes

Yip! Bark! Awoo! The eerie calls of coyotes echo through the night. Howling coyotes aren't just trying to sound spooky—they're communicating! What are they saying? Like wolves and dogs, coyotes are part of a group called canines. And as canines go, coyotes are pretty noisy.

Their scientific name, *Canis latrans,* means "barking dog." In late winter and early spring, when coyotes are finding mates and settling down, they'll gather together to make loud yip-howls. Males make long howls and females add shorter howls and yips. Younger coyotes may join in, too. The sounds help the family say, "Hey, we live here! Everybody else should back off!"

If a coyote feels threatened by a nearby animal, it'll make a huffing sound. If the threat is farther away, the coyote barks. To say hi to a family member, a coyote sings *woo-oo-wow!* So the next time you're out at night, listen for these chatty canines.

The **WORD** "coyote" comes **FROM THE AZTEC WORD** for the animal, "coyotl."

Coyotes are **BIGGER THAN FOXES** but smaller than wolves.

Coyotes can have **15 OR MORE PUPPIES AT A TIME.**

Dolphinstagram

red_fox
📍 All around the world

♥ **94 likes**

red_fox Tonight, I'll head out on the hunt—but I'm not hoping to fill my own stomach. I'll bring my catch back to the burrow, where my mate and kits are waiting for their dinner. I have a whopping 10 hungry pups, so wish me good hunting! #DadLife

CRITTER CHAT

Just_Lion_Around
Is everybody ready for my dawn *ROARRR*?

True_Stripes
Hey, have you thought of trying other sounds?

Just_Lion_Around
Like what?

True_Stripes
Well, we zebras bark and snort!

RapidCat
Cheetahs chirp, purr, and coo.

Just_Lion_Around

Well, I tried to make cheetah and zebra sounds, but the other lions laughed at me. Anyone else have communication tips?

NeckAndNeck

We male giraffes settle our differences by whacking our necks into each other until somebody gives up and runs away.

SELFIE!

Just_Lion_Around

That sounds like a literal pain in the neck. #ow

TURN PAGE ●●●

6:01 p.m.

Just_Lion_Around
It's almost roaring time. After careful consideration, I've decided that the most fun way to communicate is ... whacking my neck against another lion's neck.

 **RapidCat**
Whew!

 **Just_Lion_Around**
Just kidding! It's roaring. I was LIE-on. Get it? Lion?

 **NeckAndNeck**
...

True_Stripes
...

 **Just_Lion_Around**
ROARRRR!!

158

yowl

bon appetit!

Army Ant Colony
Ocellated_antbird
★ ★ ★ ★ ☆

This army ant colony is a powerful force. Thousands of fierce ants travel as a single stream, chasing away everything in their path. I follow them and snap up the tasty bugs they stir up. It's delicious destruction!

160

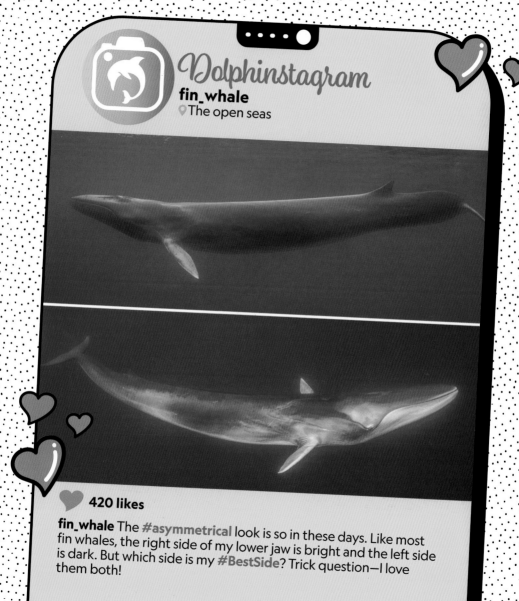

Dolphinstagram

fin_whale
📍The open seas

❤️ **420 likes**

fin_whale The #asymmetrical look is so in these days. Like most fin whales, the right side of my lower jaw is bright and the left side is dark. But which side is my #BestSide? Trick question—I love them both!

Dolphinstagram

rusty_spotted_cat
📍 India and Sri Lanka

💜 **27 likes**

rusty_spotted_cat I'm cute but fierce! I may be one of the smallest wild cats, weighing just a couple of pounds (one kilogram), but I'm a ferocious hunter. So watch out, because I'm coming for your tasty birds, rodents, lizards—and your heart! #FeelingCute

165

CRITTER CHAT

SEA OTTER

LIVES IN: California kelp forests
SCREEN NAME: YouOtterKnow

FRIENDS

JustAFluke
Gray whale

StayGolden
Garibaldi fish

Free_Hugs
Giant Pacific octopus

TURN PAGE

YouOtterKnow

Everyone says that rainforests are so pretty, but they're overrated. Kelp forests are the best! Our "trees" are 100-foot (30-m)-tall algae that sway in the current!

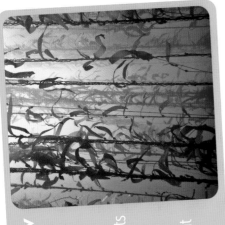

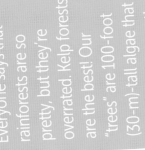

JustAFluke

Agreed! Also, whales can't swim through rainforests.

StayGolden

You forgot the best part: Kelp forests have the prettiest wildlife. See me.

SELFIE!

YouOtterKnow

I just caught the tastiest clam! Time to crack it open with my favorite rock, Mr. Lumpy. I keep him in my armpit.

StayGolden

You named your rock?

Free_Hugs

Ha! I don't need tools to eat my dinner. I've got a super sharp beak that punctures prey.

JustAFluke

That's nothing! I gulp whole mouthfuls of sand and extract food with my baleen teeth.

StayGolden

Um, I just nibble worms. But have I mentioned I'm very pretty?

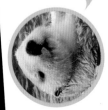

YouOtterKnow
FYI, you should thank me for keeping our forest healthy. I chow down on sea urchins that would eat the kelp.

Free_Hugs
Thank you, YouOtterKnow!

JustAFluke
Yeah, thanks, buddy! I love to hide from hungry orcas in the kelp.

StayGolden
Thanks for preserving the green backdrop that makes my colors pop! Oh, and thanks to ME for being so pretty.

YouOtterKnow
We're all grateful for your hard work, StayGolden.

169

blast! another wrong turn!

YiPadvisor

Arctic_tern
Pacific Kelp Forests

These kelp forests are pretty. The rockfish rock and the otters are otterly adorable. There's just one problem. I DIDN'T MEAN TO WIND UP IN A PACIFIC KELP FOREST!

I can't believe I'm lost again. This trip has really taken a tern. Next time, I'm going to memorize the directions instead of just winging it!

Member for 2 years

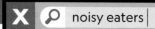

CRAFTY
COMMUNICATOR
caterpillars

Caterpillars may not seem like communicators. They tend to sit quietly on plants, munching on leaves. But if you listen closely, you'll hear them make a surprising range of sounds, from squeaks to clicks to groans!

Some caterpillars make noise to scare away predators. When a bird tries to eat a walnut sphinx moth caterpillar, the caterpillar lets out a burst of whistles. *Fweeeep! Fweeeep!* Shocked, the hungry bird flies away. Who wouldn't find a whistling caterpillar surprising?

Other caterpillars just chat among themselves. Masked birch moth caterpillars scrape their butts on leaves, creating rumbling vibrations that travel through the plant. The vibrations help them find each other so they can work together and build a shelter that keeps them safe.

And when gypsy moth caterpillars feed high in the trees, you can sometimes hear their hard poop—called frass—hitting the leaves as it falls. It's like a dry rainstorm. Eww.

MOST caterpillars **EAT PLANTS,** but **SOME** of them **EAT BUGS!**

All caterpillars grow up to be **EITHER BUTTERFLIES OR MOTHS.**

Some **MOTH** caterpillars **LIVE UNDER-WATER.**

Dolphinstagram

okapi

📍 Ituri Rainforest, Central Africa

 420 likes

okapi Some people call me a zebra giraffe because I love blending styles. I'm closely related to giraffes, but my legs are stripy like a zebra's. My combo is so cool, you'll want to o-COPY it!
#WildStyleInspo

6:39 a.m.

Grizz_Kid
I'm baffled. A human just called me a "brown bear," and another one said I was a "bruin." Pick a name, humans!

FancyAntlers
Humans are so confused. European humans call moose "elk." That's *my* name!

YouHerdMe
Lots of humans call me a "buffalo," but technically I'm a bison.

Howl_n_Prowl
Most humans just call me "AAAH GO AWAY!"

Grizz_Kid
Time for this fierce predator to FEAST!

Howl_n_Prowl
What's on the menu today?

Grizz_Kid
Um ... huge mouthfuls of moths.

Howl_n_Prowl
Moths??

Grizz_Kid
They're really high in fat! Moths are an important part of a grizzly's diet. We don't just eat deer and salmon, you know.

 **YouHerdMe**
Hey Grizz_Kid, be careful hunting those moths! I hear they're VICIOUS.

TURN PAGE

Grizz_Kid
I wish some humans didn't hate wild predators so much. We may seem scary, but we keep the ecosystem working!

Howl_n_Prowl
Definitely! We wolves may even help keep elk from eating all the plants.

FancyAntlers
True. If I didn't have to worry about wolves, I'd eat the whole park.

Grizz_Kid
FancyAntlers, if you made Yellowstone into a barren brown mess, I'd give you a piece of my mind!

FancyAntlers
You don't scare me, moth-eater!

Dolphinstagram

spider_tailed_horned_viper
📍The rocky desert of Iran

 212 likes

spider_tailed_horned_viper This is a message to all the birds out there: I'm a harmless, tasty spider and definitely NOT a venomous snake trying to attract a spider-eating bird with my tail so I can eat it. Fly on over, birds!

179

#bffs

BEAST | FRIENDS | FUREVER

Brown-throated Sloth & Sloth Moths
● Online from Central and South America

You may think our friendship is yucky. My moth BFFs live on me and help me grow algae on my fur that I slurp up for a snack. The moths' caterpillars eat my poop, too. Hey, don't judge. Friendship comes in all sizes—and smells! #BFFs

LIKE | COMMENT

CRAFTY
COMMUNICATOR

vervet monkeys

A troop of fuzzy gray vervet monkeys is chowing down on leaves in a Tanzanian woodland. Suddenly, one of them sees a hungry predator. Time to warn the others! There's just one problem: Plenty of different critters hunt vervet monkeys.

The monkeys need to tell one another—fast—whether to look around on the ground for a python, climb a tree to avoid a leopard, or hide in the brush to avoid an eagle. Luckily, vervets have a secret weapon. They make different calls for each type of predator. If they see a snake, they let loose some high-pitched chitters. These sounds tell their friends to stand on their hind legs and search the ground. For a leopard, they breathe in and out fast, making a sneezy sound. If a vervet hears this sound, it runs into a tree! For an eagle, they grunt low, saying, "Hey, keep your eyes on the skies." This is an amazing—and lifesaving—secret code.

Vervets spend a **LOT OF TIME GROOMING** and cleaning each other.

A **BABY** vervet spends its first **WEEKS HANGING ON** to its **MOM'S BELLY.**

Vervets **EAT PLANTS, SEEDS, AND FRUITS,** but they'll also snack on insects.

Dolphinstagram

strawberry_squid
Upper ocean waters

❤️ **45 likes**

strawberry_squid Hey @fin_whale, I saw your post about your #BestSide, I'm #assymetrical too! My right eye is small and blue, and my left eye is big, yellow, and points up. I can look up and down at the same time! Which side is my #BestSide? Trick question—I love them both!

185

Dolphinstagram

scimitar-horned_oryx
📍 Northern Africa

 20 likes

scimitar-horned_oryx Check out these horns! They're three feet (1 m) long and curved like a scimitar (a kind of sword). It's no wonder ancient humans might have mistaken oryx horns for unicorn horns! If you look at me from the side, you'll only see one horn! The magic is real. #WildStyleInspo

Dolphinstagram

palm_cockatoo
📍 Cape York Peninsula, Australia

 421 likes

palm_cockatoo Come to my drum concert next Tuesday at the hollow eucalyptus tree! What am I playing? I made a drumstick out of a branch, and I whack it against the tree. When I'm really feeling the groove, I start whistling super loud. Bring earplugs.

CRITTER CHAT

Shore_Thing
WARNING: Here comes low tide! Try not to dry out in the sun or get eaten by birds. I think I just saw a hungry arctic tern fly by.

RockStar
Low tide already? Yikes! TideRider, you'd better hurry up and swim back to the pool!

TideRider
I'm flapping my fins as hard as I can! #FastFish

Shore_Thing
Is everybody OK? I'm closed up tight so I won't lose water.

WellShelled
I'm safe in my shell, and I've shut the door.

TideRider
I'm in a nice wet crevice. Luckily, I can breathe air if the water gets too low!

Shore_Thing
TideRider, you have so many cool abilities! Are you going to tell me that you can fly, too?

TideRider
Only if a seagull swallows me.

TURN PAGE
• • •

Shore_Thing
The water's rising again. We survived! Use your tentacles to pat yourself on the back!

TideRider
I'm clapping my fins!

RockStar
I may be the only sea star here, but you're all stars to me.

WellShelled
Life on the coast can be so dramatic. I'm feeling a wave of emotion.

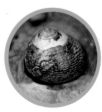

yowl

a worthy throne

Giant Malaysian Pitcher Plant
Mountain_treeshrew

★★★★★

Sometimes I'm hiking far from home when I hear the call of nature. This plant is the best place to poop! It has a comfortable bowl shape, and it even makes nectar, so I can dine while I defecate. Plus, it recycles my poo as fertilizer. It's the perfect species for my feces.

ANIMAL INFLUENCER

JOEY

SPECIES
Sea otter

FAVORITE FOOD
Ice cubes

WHY HE'S POPULAR
He's super cute.

Back in July of 2020, a woman on Canada's Vancouver Island heard a squeaky cry coming from the shore. She followed the sound and found an orphaned sea otter pup. The ball of fluff weighed just 3.8 pounds (1.7 kg).

Vancouver's Marine Mammal Rescue Centre swooped in. The facility is part of the Vancouver Aquarium, which rescues, rehabilitates, and—whenever possible—releases animals back into the wild. Staff took in the pup, now named Joey, and raised him. It wasn't easy. Rescuers had to teach Joey to swim and even to groom himself, which is tricky when you've got the thickest fur in the animal kingdom.

Through it all, Joey wasn't alone. He had other young sea otters to play with, but he also had thousands of human friends watching him on a video feed. Later, Joey moved to the Vancouver Aquarium. Viewers now tune in to the aquarium's feed to cheer him on as he splashes, plays, and crunches his favorite treat: ice cubes!

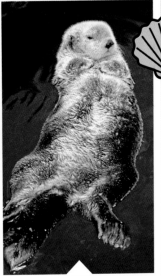

Joey **SUCKS ON HIS PAW** when he is sleepy.

Sea otters **RARELY COME ONTO LAND.**

Sea otters **USE TOOLS LIKE ROCKS** to smash shells and eat the meat inside.

Dolphinstagram

eastern_black-and-white_colobus_monkey
📍 Central Africa

 59 likes

eastern_black-and-white_colobus_monkey Yes, my tail is beautiful, but it's more than just a fashion accessory. It's also a lifesaver! When I leap, my tail acts as a parachute, slowing my fall and making sure I land safely. My tail's got my back! #Tailfie

home sssweet home

Eastern_indigo_snake
Gopher Tortoise Burrow
🐾 🐾 🐾 🐾 🐾

Member for 2 years

Gopher tortoise burrows are popular in my neck of the woods. They're home to tortoises, but also to frogs, mice, burrowing owls, rattlesnakes, and more! This particular burrow is a great place to hang out. It keeps me cool on hot days and safe from forest fires.

So why am I giving this burrow four stars instead of five? Well, I can tell that the last occupant was a skunk. I mean, I can SMELL that the last occupant was a skunk. Yuck!

Giant Moray Eel & Pacific Cleaner Shrimp
● Online from the Pacific Ocean

As a moray eel, it's important that I look and feel my best. My shrimp BFF nips parasites off my skin. What does she get out of the ordeel? A tasty meel! She even puts up with all my eel puns. Our friendship is the reel deel!
#BFFs

| LIKE | COMMENT |

TalkToTheClaw

SPECIES: Banana fiddler crab
LIKES: The color yellow
DISLIKES: Hungry gulls, other male banana fiddler crabs

ABOUT ME: I live on a patch of sand and sleep in a damp burrow. My life may not be luxurious, but I've got something special: one giant yellow claw that I wave around! It's clawsome. It's clawspicious. It's claw-inspiring. Listen, I sit on the damp sand all day so I have a lot of time to think up claw puns.

pick me!

connect with me!

201

Every year on February 2, thousands of people come from miles away and gather at a place called Gobbler's Knob in Punxsutawney, Pennsylvania, U.S.A., and wait for a man in a tuxedo and top hat to make an announcement. What will the fancily dressed man share with the crowd? A weather prediction from a 20-pound (9-kg) squirrel. Seriously.

The star of the show, Punxsutawney Phil, is a groundhog (basically, a big ground squirrel). According to legend, if a groundhog emerges from its den and sees its shadow on February 2, there will be six more weeks of winter. If it doesn't, then spring is on its way. Punxsutawney Phil wakes up and "speaks" with an inner circle of tuxedo-clad humans. They interpret his "words" (OK, so there's a little imagination going on here) and announce whether Phil saw his shadow.

Phil is only right about 40 percent of the time, so this whole thing is a bit silly. But it's also fun. People enjoy a day of music, food, and groundhoggy good times.

PUNXSUTAWNEY PHIL

SPECIES
Groundhog

FAVORITE FOOD
Carrots

WHY HE'S POPULAR
He predicts the weather—sort of.

Groundhogs **HIBERNATE,** resting and not eating, for as long as **HALF A YEAR.**

During **PARADES,** Phil **RIDES** in a **SPECIAL BUS** called the **PHILMOBILE.**

Groundhog **TEETH** are **CHISEL-LIKE,** and they **NEVER STOP GROWING.**

CRITTER CHAT

ARCTIC TERN

LIVES IN: The Antarctic in the winter
(later, she'll travel to the Arctic!)
SCREEN NAME: TernAround

FRIENDS

SnowSquawker
Chinstrap penguin

BlubberButt
Weddell seal

WinglessWonder
Antarctic midge

TernAround
Hi, friends! I'm FINALLY back in Antarctica! I can't believe I made it. Would you believe I flew nearly 20,000 miles (32,000 km)?

SnowSquawker
Wow, that's a lot of flapping! FYI, I think flying is overrated.

WinglessWonder
I agree. Most midges have wings, but we Antarctic midges don't need them. Our babies burrow underground!
#WhateverKeepsMeWarm

TernAround
But flying is so fun, and it lets me see the world! Even if I sometimes get lost and see more of it than I'd like ...

TURN PAGE
● ● ●

205

TernAround
I just caught a tasty fish! But *brr*, that water sure is cold. Friends who spend all day swimming, how do you stay warm?

BlubberButt
A third of my body is made of blubber that acts like a cozy blanket. I can dive 2,000 feet (610 m) down and still stay toasty!

SnowSquawker
I've got blubber, too! Plus, my thick feathers keep me warm.

TernAround
I see. How FATscinating!

2:42 p.m.

10:07 p.m.

TernAround
What's something that makes you special? I'll start: I've got the longest migration of any animal!

WinglessWonder
I'm the only insect in Antarctica.

BlubberButt
I'm the world's southernmost seal species.

SnowSquawker
My poop enriches the soil, nourishing plants and lichen that feed millions of small creatures and keep the ecosystem working. #SuperPoop

TernAround
That's ... ew. That's definitely special.

YOU'VE REACHED **THE TAIL END** OF THIS BOOK.

Thanks for **tern-ing** all these pages and meeting so many **pun-derful animals.** If you'd like, you can **migrate back to page one** and fly through it all again!

Boldface indicates illustrations.

A

American bison 68–69, **68–69**, 90–93, **90–93**, 176–177, **176–177**
American robins 42–45, **42–45**
Antarctic midges 204–207, **204–207**
Arctic foxes 6–9, **6–9**, 56, **56**
Arctic terns 4–9, **4–9**, 51, **51**, 171, **171**, 204–209, **204–209**
Army ants 159, **159**
Atlantic spotted dolphins 126, **126**
Aye-ayes 80–83, **80–83**

B

Baird's tapirs 70–73, **70–73**
Bamboo 132, 133, 135, **135**
Banana fiddler crabs 201, **201**
Banded mongooses 97, **97**
Bat stars 100–103, **100–103**, 190–192, **190–192**
Bats 22, **22**, 57, **57**
Bears
    black bears 10, **10**
    grizzly bears 90–93, **90–93**, 176–178, **176–178**
    polar bears 56, **56**
Bengal tigers 144, **144**
Black bears 10, **10**
Black-capped chickadees 76–77, **77**
Black turban snails 100–102, **100–102**

Blowflies 59, **59**
Bold jumping spiders 24–27, **24–27**
Brilliant-thighed poison frogs 130, **130**
Brown-throated sloths 181, **181**
Budgerigars 16–19, **16–19**
Buffalo. *see* American bison
Butterflies 70–73, **70–73**, 173

C

Camels **40–41**, 164, **164**
Capybaras 120, **120**, **170**
Caterpillars 128, **128**, 172–173, **173**
Cheetahs 32–35, **32–35**, 156–158, **156–158**
Chinstrap penguins 204–207, **204–207**
Clouded leopards 74, **74**
Clownfish 139, **139**
Coyotes 152–153, **153**
Crabs **160**
    banana fiddler crabs 201, **201**
    graceful decorator crabs 116, **116**
    hydrothermal vent crabs 146–149, **146–149**
Cuvier's beaked whales 28, **28**

D

Dead horse arum lilies 59, **59**
Deathstalker scorpions 22, **22**
Desert long-eared bats 22, **22**
Dogs 24–27, **24–27**, 152
Dolphins 46–47, **46–47**, 126, **126**, 141, **141**
Dromedary camels 164, **164**
Dumbo octopuses 14, **14**

E

Earthworms 122–125, **122–125**
Eastern black-and-white colobus monkeys 196, **196**

Eastern indigo snakes 197, **197**
Eastern spadefoot toads 137, **137**
Elephants 95, **142–143**
Elk 90–93, **90–93**, 176, **176**, 178, **178**

F

Fin whales 161, **161**
Fireflies 20–21, **21**
Flamboyant cuttlefish 136, **136**
Forest giant owl butterflies 70–73, **70–73**

G

Garibaldi fish 166–169, **166–169**
Giant clams 146–149, **146–149**
Giant green anemones 100–103, **100–103**,
 190–192, **190–192**
Giant Malaysian pitcher plants 193, **193**
Giant moray eels 200, **200**
Giant Pacific octopuses 166–169, **166–169**
Giant pandas 132–135, **132–135**
Giant tube worms 146–149, **146–149**
Giraffes **32**, 34, **34**, 88, **88**, 157, **157**
Goblin sharks 50, **50**
Golden pheasants 132–135, **132–135**
Golden snub-nosed monkeys 132–135, **132–135**
Golden takins 132–135, **132–135**
Gopher tortoise burrows 197, **197**
Graceful decorator crabs 116, **116**
Gray squirrels 42–45, **42–45**
Gray whales 166–169, **166–169**
Gray wolves 90–93, **90–93**, 109, **109**, 176–178,
 176–178
Great white sharks 52–55, **52–55**, 110–112, **110–112**
Greater bilbies 16–19, **16–19**
Greater rheas 66, **66**

Green sea turtles 52–55, **52–55**, 111, **111**
Grizzly bears **90–93**, 90–93, 176–178, **176–178**
Groundhogs 202–203, **202–203**

H

Hippopotamuses 94, 140–141, **140–141**
Honduran white bats 57, **57**
Hooded seals 67, **67**
House cats **180**
House mice 37, **37**
House wrens 30, **30**
Humpback whales 12–13, **12–13**
Hydrothermal vent crabs 146–149, **146–149**

I

Iguanas **118–119**
Indris 80–83, **80–83**

J

Japanese dwarf flying squirrels 98, **98**
Jellyfish 36, **36**, 111
Jorunna parva 145, **145**

K

Kangaroos 16–19, **16–19**
Kelp forests 167, **167**, 171, **171**
King penguins 106–107, **106–107**
Koalas 78, **78**

L

Laysan albatrosses 38–39, **38–39**
Lemon sharks 131, **131**
Lemurs 80–83, **80–83**
Leopard geckos 113, **113**
Lions **32–25**, 32–35, 156–158, **156–158**
Live sharksuckers 131, **131**

M

Madame Berthe's mouse lemurs 80–83, **80–83**
Magnificent sea anemones 139, **139**
Malayan tapirs 15, **15**
Mantled howler monkeys 70–73, **70–73**
Mice 37, **37,** 197
Milkweed 128, **128**
Monarch caterpillars 128, **128**
Monkeys
    black-and-white colobus monkeys 196, **196**
    golden snub-nosed monkeys 132–135,
        132–135
    mantled howler monkeys 70–73, **70–73**
    vervet monkeys 182–183, **182–183**
Moose 109, 176
Moths 75, **75,** 172, 173, 177, 181, **181**
Mountain gorillas 60, **60**
Mountain treeshrews 193, **193**
Mule deer 117, **117**
Musk oxen 6–9, **6–9**

N

Naked mole rats 62–65, **62–65**
Narwhals 6–9, **6–9,** 105, **105**
Northern elephant seals 52–55, **52–55,** 112, **112**
Northern mockingbirds 42–45, **42–45**
Northern pudus 61, **61**

O

Ocellated antbirds 159, **159**
Octopuses 14, **14,** 166–169, **166–169**
Okapis 175, **175**
Opossums 49, **49**
Orcas 46–47, **46–47**
Orchid bees 96, **96**

Orchid mantises 23, **23**
Otters **48,** 166–169, **166–169,** 194–195, **194–195**
Owls 76, **174,** 197

P

Pacific cleaner shrimp 200, **200**
Palm cockatoos 188, **188**
Pancake tortoises 138, **138**
Peacock spiders 127, **127**
Penguins
    chinstrap penguins 204–207, **204–207**
    king penguins 106–107, **106–107**
Plains zebras 29, **29, 32,** 34, **34,** 156–158, **156–158**
Platypuses 11, **11**
Poison frogs 114–115, **114–115,** 130, **130**
Polar bears 56, **56**

R

Rabbits 94, 108, **108,** 189
Raccoons 42–45, **42–45,** 76
Rainbow agamas 150, **150**
Rattail fish 146–149, **146–149**
Red foxes 154, **154**
Red kangaroos 16–19, **16–19**
Remoras 131, **131**
Resplendent quetzals 70-73, **70–73**
Rhinoceroses 94–95, **94–95**
Ring-tailed lemurs 80–83, **80–83**
Rusty-spotted cats 165, **165**

S

Scarlet macaws 85, **85**
Scimitar-horned oryx 187, **187**
Sea otters 166–169, **166–169,** 194–195, **194–195**
Sea slugs 145, **145**

Sea stars 100–103, **100–103,** 190–192, **190–192**
Sea turtles 52–55, **52–55, 58,** 111, **111**
Seals
    hooded seals 67, **67**
    northern elephant seals 52–55, **52–55,** 112, **112**
    Weddell seals 204–207, **204–207**
Servals 62–65, **62–65**
Sharks
    goblin sharks 50, **50**
    great white sharks 52–55, **52–55,** 110–112, **110–112**
    lemon sharks 131, **131**
    whale sharks 79, **79**
Silverfish 24–27, **24–27**
Sloth moths 181, **181**
Smooth earth snakes 122–125, **122–125**
Snakes
    eastern indigo snakes 197, **197**
    smooth earth snakes 122–125, **122–125**
    spider-tailed horned vipers 179, **179**
    timber rattlesnakes 104, **104**
Snow leopards 121, **121**
Sperm whales 52–55, **52–55,** 110–112, **110–112**
Spider-tailed horned vipers 179, **179**
Spiders 24–27, **24–27,** 125, 127, **127**
Spotted salamanders 122–125, **122–125**
Star-nosed moles 122–125, **122–125**
Strawberry squid 184, **184**

T
Thorny devils 16–19, **16–19**
Three-wattled bellbirds 186, **186**
Tidepool sculpins 100–103, **100–103,** 190–192, **190–192**

Timber rattlesnakes 104, **104**
Turkey vultures 89, **89**

U
Upside-down jellyfish 36, **36**

V
Varied carpet beetles 24–27, **24–27**
Vervet monkeys 182–183, **182–183**
Virginia opossums 49, **49**
Volcano rabbits 108, **108**

W
Warthogs 62–65, **62–65,** 97, **97**
Weddell seals 204–207, **204–207**
Western grebes 151, **151**
Whale sharks 79, **79**
Whales
    Cuvier's beaked whales 28, **28**
    fin whales 161, **161**
    gray whales 166–169, **166–169**
    humpback whales 12–13, **12–13**
    sperm whales 110–112, **110–112**
Whistling thorn trees 88, **88**
White rhinoceroses 94–95, **94–95**

Y
Yellow-billed oxpeckers 29, **29**
Yellow caracaras 120, **120**
Yellow peach moths 75, **75**

Z
Zebras 29, **29, 32,** 34, **34, 142–143,** 156–158, **156–158**

ASP: Alamy Stock Photo; DR: Dreamstime; GI: Getty Images; MP: Minden Pictures; SS: Shutterstock

Cover (giraffe), prapass/SS; (phone), cobalt88/SS; (dog), GlobalP/GI; (paw), JacobWelsh/SS; (microphone), kak2s/SS; (mouse), creativenature.nl/Adobe Stock; Back cover (hyena), Daniel-Alvarez/SS; (lizard), Chase D'animulls/SS; 1, African Safari Collection/ASP; 2, Kuritafsheen/DR; 3, Bill Gozansky/ASP; 4-5, Buiten-Beeld/Paul van Hoof/ASP; 6-9 (tern), Gail Johnson/Adobe Stock; 6-9 (narwhal), Doc White/ardea/age fotostock; 6-9 (musk ox), FugeSpot/GI; 6-9 (arctic fox), Karine Patry/DR; 7 (musk ox calf), Naturablichter/DR; 8 (arctic foxes), guenterguni/GI; 10 (UP), junah666/Adobe Stock; 10 (LO), georgesanker/ASP; 11, Dave Watts/Newscom; 12 (BOTH), Craig Parry; 13 (UP LE), Craig Parry; 13 (UP RT), Sean Steininger/SS; 13 (LO), Paul Souders/Worldfoto/MP; 14, Dante Fenolio/Science Photo Library; 15 (UP LE), Yatra/SS; 15 (UP RT), RavindranJohn Smith/GI; 15 (LO), Jonah Goh/SS; 16-19 (kangaroo), Theo Allofs/MP; 16-19 (thorny devil), Janelle Lugge/SS; 16-19 (greater bilby), Martin Withers/MP; 16-19 (budgerigar), Tracey Heimberger/SS; 18 (flock of birds), Chris Watson/SS; 18 (bilby portrait), Roland Seitre/Nature Picture Library; 19 (paws), JacobWelsh/SS; 21 (UP LE), khlungcenter/SS; 21 (UP RT), Jeff J Daly/ASP; 21 (LO), higrace photo/GI; 22 (LE), Brock Fenton; 22 (RT), Aitivamon/SS; 22 (BACKGROUND), Vojko Kavcic/SS; 23, Sebastian Janicki/SS; 24-27 (spider), Jes_Abeita/GI; 24-27 (beetle), ANP Photo/age fotostock; 24-27 (silverfish), H. Bellmann/F. Hecker/Blickwinkel/age fotostock; 24-27 (dog), Africa Studio/SS; 28, Todd Pusser/Nature Picture Library/ASP; 29 (UP LE), Anan Kaewkhammul/SS; 29 (UP RT), Art Wolfe/Science Photo Library; 29 (LO), Steffen Foerster/DR; 30 (bird), geraldmarella/Adobe Stock; 30 (walking stick bug), Eric Isselee/SS; 30 (sticks), xpixel/SS; 31, Cathy Keifer/Adobe Stock; 32-35 (lion), Buffy1982/SS; 32-35 (zebra), Johan Swanepoel/SS; 32-35 (cheetah), bearerofchrist/GI; 32-35 (giraffe), Arisa/Adobe Stock; 34 (giraffe eating), Koverninska Olga/SS; 35 (paws), Nagel Photography/SS; 36, Pete Oxford/MP; 37 (mouse, both), Rudmer Zwerver/SS; 37 (microphone), kak2s/SS; 38 (BOTH), USFWS Photo/ASP; 39 (UP LE), USFWS Photo/ASP; 39 (UP RT), Heather Angel/Natural Visions/ASP; 39 (LO), Tui De Roy/MP/Newscom; 40-41, Susy Baels/SS; 42-45 (robin), Susan Helmuth/GI; 42-45 (raccoon), jadimages/SS; 42-45 (squirrel), RMVera/Adobe Stock; 42-45 (mockingbird), drferry/GI; 43 (robin on branch), Brian Guest/SS; 46, Gerard Lacz/MP; 47 (UP LE), Anne-Marie Palmer/ASP; 47 (UP RT), WaterFrame_fba/ASP; 47 (LO), Christopher Swann/MP; 48, Scooperdigital/DR; 49, Evelyn D. Harrison/SS; 50, David Shen/Blue Planet Archive; 51 (UP), Alexander Erdbeer/Adobe Stock; 51 (LO RT), Dennis van de Wate/SS; 51 (LO LE), Gail Johnson/Adobe Stock; 52-55 (shark), Ramon Carretero/DR; 52-55 (whale), Michael Nolan/age fotostock; 52-55 (seal), Sheila Fitzgerald/ASP; 52-55 (sea turtle), ShaneMyersPhoto/GI; 53 (shark open mouth), Martin Prochazkacz/SS; 54 (shark selfie), Wildestanimal/ASP; 55 (shark breaching), Gary Bell/Oceanwide Images; 56 (UP RT), Iakov Filimonov/SS; 56 (UP LE), Karine Patry/DR; 56 (LO LE), DmitryND/GI; 56 (LO RT), schuie/GI; 57, Konrad Wothe/MP; 58, Richard Carey/DR; 59 (UP), Miles Barton/MP; 59 (LO), zhang yongxin/age fotostock; 60 (UP), olga_gl/SS; 60 (LO), guenterguni/GI; 61, ullstein bild/GI; 62-65 (naked mole rat in tunnel), Frans Lanting/MINT Images/Science Source; 62-65 (serval), Koilee/SS; 62-65 (naked mole rat portrait), Hans-Juergen Koch/MP; 62-65 (warthog), Stefonlinton/GI; 64 (naked mole rats), blickwinkel/Schmidbauer/ASP; 66, John Waters/Nature Picture Library; 67 (UP LE), Gerard Lacz/age fotostock; 67 (UP RT), Enrique/Adobe Stock; 67 (LO), M. Watson/ardea Collection/Mary Evans Picture Library Ltd/age fotostock; 68 (LE), Jillian Cain/DR; 68 (RT), Doug Pensinger/GI; 69 (UP RT), Marcia Straub/GI; 69 (UP LE), Doug Pensinger/GI; 69 (LO), O.S. Fisher/SS; 70-73 (tapir), Mark_Kostich/SS; 70-73 (monkey), Mark Newman/GI; 70-73 (butterfly), TXJules/GI; 70-73 (quetzal), Greg Basco/MP; 71 (quetzal in tree), Bill Baston/MP; 72 (monkey howling), David Tipling/Universal Images Group/Education Images/GI; 73 (puma), ian600f/GI; 74, Sylvain Cordier/GI; 75 (UP LE), Muhammad Shafiq; 75 (UP RT), Cheryl E. Davis/SS; 75 (LO), Matee Nuserm/SS; 77 (UP LE), ND700/SS; 77 (UP RT), Scott Leslie/MP; 77 (LO), Larry Michae/MP; 78 (UP), Luca Santilli/SS; 78 (LO), Juergen & Christine Sohns/MP; 79, Krzysztof Odziomek/DR; 80-83 (ring-tailed lemur), Appfind/GI; 80-83 (mouse lemur), Mark Carwardine/MP; 80-83 (indri), Damian322/DR; 80-83 (aye-aye), javarman3/GI; 81 (aye-aye selfie), Thorsten Negro/GI; 83 (aye-aye fingers), Konrad Wothe/MP; 84, Karl Terblanche/ardea/age fotostock; 85 (UP), Mario Wong Pastor/SS; 85 (LO LE), Martin Mecnarowsk/SS; 85 (LO RT), Murray Cooper/MP; 86-87, Riza Arif Pratama/DR; 88 (LE), Przemyslaw Skibinsk/SS; 88 (UP RT), prapass/SS; 88 (LO RT), Robert Winslow/age fotostock; 89, Patricio Robles Gil/MP; 90-93 (bear), Andy Rouse/Nature Picture Library/Alamy; 90-93 (wolf), Zoonar/Jearu/ASP; 90-93 (bison), Tim Fitzharris/MP; 90-93 (elk), Betty4240/DR; 91 (sign), Ingo70/SS; 92 (tourist), Wollertz/DR; 93 (paws), berkay/GI; 94, digidreamgrafix/SS; 95 (UP LE), Nobby Clarke/SS; 95 (UP RT), Jurgens Potgiete/SS; 95 (LO), Francois van Heerden/SS; 96 (UP), Ivan Kurmyshov/SS; 96 (LO), Lucasmeirelles94/DR; 97 (LO), Anup Shah/MP; 97 (UP LE), Stefonlinton/GI; 97 (UP RT), Wrangel/DR; 98, Tony Wu/MP; 99, Roberto Barilani/GI; 100-103 (anemone), Georgette Douwma/MP; 100-103 (sculpin), Stuart Wilson/Science Source; 100-103 (snail), Paul Bersebach/

MediaNews Group/Orange County Register/GI; 100-103 (sea star), feathercollector/Adobe Stock; 102 (anemone detail), Jeff Rotman/GI; 103 (sea star detail), Jeffrey Rotman/MP; 104, Paul Williams/ASP; 105 (UP), Oleg/SS; 105 (LO), Paul Nicklen/GI; 106 (BOTH), Jane Barlow/ASP; 107 (UP LE), Jane Barlow/ASP; 107 (UP RT), Rhinie van Meurs/MP; 107 (LO), Isabella Pfenninger/SS; 108 (UP LE), George D. Lepp/GI; 108 (LO LE), Claudio Contreras/Nature Picture Library/ASP; 108 (RT), Max Rastello/SS; 109 (LE), David Osborn/SS; 109 (RT), Gerry Ellis/MP; 110-112 (shark), Ramon Carretero/DR; 110-112 (whale), Michael Nolan/age fotostock; 111-112 (sea turtle), ShaneMyersPhoto/GI; 112 (seal), Sheila Fitzgerald/ASP; 113, mzphoto11/Adobe Stock; 114, Brad Wilson/DVM/GI; 115 (UP LE), Paul A. Souders/GI; 115 (UP RT), kikkerdirk/GI; 115 (LO), reptiles4all/GI; 116, Andrey Nekrasov/imageBROKER/age fotostock; 117 (UP LE), JHWilliams/GI; 117 (UP RT), Straystone/GI; 117 (LO), twildlife/GI; 118-119, Huy Thoai/DR; 120 (BOTH), Christophe Courteau/MP; 121, abzerit/GI; 122-125 (salamander), blickwinkel/Teigler/ASP; 122-125 (mole), Dembinsky Photo Assn./MP; 122-125 (snake), Guillaume Tutton/GI; 122-125 (worm), blickwinkel/FieberASP; 124 (mole selfie), Michael Habicht/age fotostock; 126, SeaTops/imageBROKER/ASP; 127 (UP LE), Adam Fletcher/MP; 127 (UP RT) Olga Selyutina/SS; 127 (LO), Jurgen Otto/SS; 128 (LE), Jason Ondreicka/iStockphoto/GI; 128 (RT), CathyKeifer/GI; 129, Andrey Gudkov/Adobe Stock; 130, Dr Morley Read/SS; 131 (UP), Cigdem Sean Cooper/SS; 131 (LO LE), Shane Gros/SS; 131 (LO RT), Frhojdysz/DR; 132-135 (monkey), Huangshuohui/DR; 132-135 (pheasant), LagunaticPhoto/GI; 132-135 (takin), Wim Wyloeck/DR; 132-135 (panda), McPhoto/age fotostock; 134 (monkey detail), Huangshuohui/DR; 135 (bamboo), knet2d/SS; 136, SeaTops/imageBROKER/ASP; 137 (LE), Jason Ross/age fotostock; 137 (RT), B. Trapp/Blickwinkel/age fotostock; 138 (UP), Steimer, C/age fotostock; 138 (LO), Malcolm Schuyl/MP; 139 (UP LE), Derek Holzapfel/DR; 139 (UP RT), Kletr/SS; 139 (LO), hansgertbroeder/GI; 140 (BOTH), WENN/age fotostock; 141 (UP LE), WENN/ASP; 141 (UP RT), WENN/ASP; 141 (LO), Melissa Schalke/SS; 142-143, Charissa Lotter/DR; 144 (UP), valeriyap/Adobe Stock; 144 (shoes), Picsfive/SS; 144 (LO), dikkyoesin1/GI; 145, kiawmanas/SS; 146-149 (tube worms), Emory Kristoff/National Geographic Image Collection; 146-149 (crab), Ralph White/GI; 146-149 (fish), Marevision/age fotostock; 146-149 (clam), Woods Hole Oceanographic Institution; 147 (tube worms detail), Ralph White/GI; 150, RFcompany/age fotostock; 151 (UP LE), Amanda Guercio/SS; 151 (UP RT), Steve Gettle/MP; 151 (LO), Danita Delimont/ASP; 153 (UP LE), JayPierstorff/SS; 153 (UP RT), Tom Mangelsen/MP; 153 (LO), Tempau/GI; 154, Saverio Gatto/ASP; 155, Sergey Korotkov/DR; 156-158 (lion), Buffy1982/SS; 156-158 (zebra), Johan Swanepoel/SS; 156-158 (cheetah), bearerofchrist/GI; 157-158 (giraffe), Arisa/Adobe Stock; 157 (giraffes fighting), Steffen Foerster/; 158 (paws), Nagel Photography/SS; 159 (UP LE), David Tipling/MP; 159 (UP RT), Christian Ziegler/MP; 159 (LO), Konrad Wothe/MP; 160, Stefan Oberhauser/oneworld picture/ASP; 161 (BOTH), wildestanimal/GI; 162-163, cdascher/GI; 164 (UP), acarapi/SS; 164 (LO), SeraphP/SS; 165, Gerard Lacz/MP; 166-169 (sea otter), heatherwest/GI; 166-169 (octopus), Andrey Nekrasov/GI; 166-169 (fish), Douglas Klug/GI; 166-169 (whale), Robert Harding Picture Library/GI; 167 (kelp), Brandon B/SS; 167 (fish portrait), Eduardo Baena/GI; 168 (whale baleen), jo Crebbin/SS; 169 (paws), Tom & Pat Leeson/Mary Evans Picture Library Ltd/age fotostock; 170, nok6716/iStockphoto/GI; 171 (UP), Uryadnikov Sergey/Adobe Stock; 171 (LO LE), Gail Johnson/Adobe Stock; 171 (LO RT), Jeff Rotman/ASP; 173 (UP LE), Hijrawan Afif/GI; 173 (UP RT), Malcolm Schuyl/MP; 173 (LO), StevenRussellSmithPhotos/SS; 174, Jim Pintar/iStockphoto/GI; 175, Gleb Ivanov/DR; 176-178 (bear), Andy Rouse/Nature Picture Library/Alamy; 176-178 (elk), Betty4240/DR; 176-178 (bison), Tim Fitzharris/MP; 176-178 (wolf), Zoonar/Jearu/ASP; 179, reptiles4all/GI; 180, points/GI; 181 (UP LE), Roland Seitre/Nature Picture Library; 181 (UP RT), Damsea/SS; 181 (LO LE), Christian Ziegler/Danita Delimont, Agent/ASP; 181 (LO RT), Damsea/SS; 182, Nigel Dennis/age fotostock; 183 (UP LE), SerkanMutan/Adobe Stock; 183 (UP RT), Stefonlinton/GI; 183 (LO), Nigel Sawyer/ASP; 184, David Shale/Nature Picture Library; 185, Norbert Wu/MP; 186 (LE), Michael and Patricia Fogden/MP; 186 (RT), HomeArt/SS; 187, Dannyiacob/GI; 188, Konrad Wothe/MP; 189, dirkvandevyver/GI; 190-192 (anemone), Georgette Douwma/MP; 190-192 (sea star), feathercollector/Adobe Stock; 190-192 (sculpin), Stuart Wilson/Science Source; 191-192 (snail), Paul Bersebach/MediaNews Group/Orange County Register/GI; 192 (anemone detail), Gerald D. Tang/DR; 193 (UP), Paul Williams/MP; 193 (LO), Chien Lee/MP; 194 (BOTH), Vancouver Aquarium; 195 (UP LE), Vancouver Aquarium; 195 (UP RT), Magryt/Adobe Stock; 195 (LO), Alan Vernon/GI; 196, Martin Grosnick/Ardea/age fotostock; 197 (UP), pete oxford/age fotostock; 197 (LO LE), Danita Delimont/ASP; 197 (LO RT), Pete Oxford/MP; 198-199, Nopadol Uengbunchoo/DR; 200 (UP LE), Georgette Douwma/GI; 200 (UP RT), marrio31/GI; 200 (LO), Claudio Dias/GI; 201 (LE), Julie Burgher; 201 (RT), Image Broker/age fotostock; 202 (LE), Mitch Shark/SS; 202 (RT), fdastudillo/GI; 203 (UP LE), Reuters/Alan Freed/ASP; 203 (UP RT), Yevgeniy Drobotenko/GI; 203 (LO), Brian E Kushner/SS; 204-207 (tern), Gail Johnson/Adobe Stock; 204-207 (seal), Sergey/Adobe Stock; 204-207 (penguin), amheruko/GI; 204-207 (midge), Richard Lee; 207 (penguins), Vadim_Nefedov/GI; 208, Winfried Wisniewski/MP

To Isaac Z. Never stop asking questions!
—Rosemary

Since 1888, the National Geographic Society has funded more than 14,000 research, conservation, education, and storytelling projects around the world. National Geographic Partners distributes a portion of the funds it receives from your purchase to National Geographic Society to support programs including the conservation of animals and their habitats. To learn more, visit natgeo.com/info.

For more information, visit national geographic.com, call 1-877-873-6846, or write to the following address:

National Geographic Partners, LLC
1145 17th Street NW
Washington, DC 20036-4688 U.S.A.

For librarians and teachers:
nationalgeographic.com/books/librarians-and-educators

More for kids from National Geographic:
natgeokids.com

For rights or permissions inquiries, please contact National Geographic Books Subsidiary Rights: bookrights@natgeo.com

Designed by Sanjida Rashid

Library of Congress Cataloging-in-Publication Data

Names: Mosco, Rosemary, author.
Title: Critter chat / Rosemary Mosco.
Description: Washington, D. C. : National Geographic Kids, [2022] I Audience: Ages 8-12. I Audience: Grades 4-6.
Identifiers: LCCN 2019055272 I ISBN 9781426371707 (paperback) I ISBN 9781426371714 (library binding)
Subjects: CYAC: Animals--Fiction. I Social media--Fiction. I Humorous stories.
Classification: LCC PZ7.1.M67717 Cri 2021 I DDC [Fic]--dc23
LC record available at https://lccn.loc.gov/2019055272

The publisher would like to thank the book team: Kathryn Williams, project editor; Lori Epstein, photo director; Alison O'Brien Muff, photo editor; Joan Gossett, editorial production manager; Anne LeongSon and Gus Tello, design production assistants; and Michelle Harris, fact-checker.

Printed in China
21/PPS/1